Tough Choices for Teachers

Ethical Challenges in Today's Schools and Classrooms

Robert Infantino and Rebecca Wilke

ROWMAN & LITTLEFIELD EDUCATION
Lanham • New York • Toronto • Plymouth, UK

Published in the United States of America
by Rowman & Littlefield Education
A Division of Rowman & Littlefield Publishers, Inc.
A wholly owned subsidary of The Rowman & Littlefield Publishing Group, Inc.
4501 Forbes Boulevard, Suite 200, Lanham, Maryland 20706
www.rowmaneducation.com

Estover Road
Plymouth PL6 7PY
United Kingdom

British Library Cataloguing in Publication Information Available

Library of Congress Cataloging-in-Publication Data
Infantino, Robert L.
   Tough choices for teachers : ethical challenges in today's schools and classrooms /
Robert Infantino and Rebecca Wilke.
      p. cm.
   Includes bibliographical references.
   ISBN 978-1-60709-085-4 (cloth : alk. paper) — ISBN 978-1-60709-086-1 (pbk. : alk.
paper) — ISBN 978-1-60709-087-8 (electronic)
   1. Teachers—Professional ethics—Case studies. 2. Teaching—Moral and ethical
aspects—Case studies. I. Wilke, Rebecca Lynn. II. Title.
   LB1779.I54 2009
   174'.937—dc22   2008049327

$\otimes$™ The paper used in this publication meets the minimum requirements of
American National Standard for Information Sciences—Permanence of
Paper for Printed Library Materials, ANSI/NISO Z39.48-1992.
Manufactured in the United States of America.

Contents

~

Preface

Thoughtful decision making should be part of every educator's daily experience. From lesson planning to instructional practice to classroom management, teachers must make choices constantly and consistently throughout the school day. Sometimes these decisions are easy—for instance, who needs to be moved to a new seat in order for the class to operate better or which math activity should be included with the next lesson for more hands-on experience for the kids. Yet, some educational decisions are difficult, requiring deliberate thought and effort, while others are much more delicate in nature—or even potentially detrimental to one's career.

What kinds of issues are we talking about? Well, you can open almost any newspaper across the country or tune into a national broadcast of the evening news to hear about problems in today's classrooms, such as misconduct by modern-day educators. In fact, some of the stories of inappropriate sexual conduct between teachers and their students have rocked the very foundation of what many Americans believed about the educational process.

While these stories sadden us, fortunately they are among the extreme scenarios of educational ethics. However, there are other ethical issues that must concern those of us who hope to maintain the high standards we have worked so hard for in our schools. Some of these concerns include

- lack of honesty and truth telling between individuals
- disregard for established rules
- misuse of time, funds, and property

- an increase in instances of plagiarism and a decrease in giving proper credit for another's written or artistic work
- inflated grades and undue pressure about grading
- inappropriate relationships between coworkers

These are just a few of the issues that today's teachers must deal with in and around their classrooms besides their already highly impacted, day-to-day teaching schedules.

Helping new and experienced teachers think more deeply about ethical dilemmas is one of the main reasons that we have written *Tough Choices for Teachers: Ethical Challenges in Today's Schools and Classrooms*. Our goal is to help you avoid some of the potential pitfalls that you may face as you interact with others in your workplace. We have included what we refer to as the "dirty dozen"—a collection of case studies based on real-life stories that we have observed in our collective six decades of experience with educators in both public and private school settings. Although we have changed the names to protect the innocent (and not-so-innocent), we can assure you that these scenarios did happen . . . and they could possibly be like ones that you might face in the not-too-distant future.

Despite the intensive training they undertake to excel in the field of education, few teachers are given the tools necessary to think through these types of ethical problems and design a decision-making process that works for them. *Tough Choices for Teachers* not only provides twelve descriptive stories that transcend grade levels but also leads you into intrapersonal and interpersonal conversations about the ethical issues impacting educators all around you. Each of the case chapters includes an introductory section we call "Initial Thoughts," followed by a case study on an ethical issue. Each case is introduced by a boxed item called "Points to Ponder," designed to stimulate your thinking before you read the case. Afterwards, a series of ideas to contemplate called "Questions for Consideration" helps guide you through the decision-making process. For instance, you may be asked things like

- What would I do if I were placed in this situation?
- How have my upbringing and culture influenced how I might act in this type of scenario?
- Would I be willing to take a stand for what is right, even if other staff members disagree?

Finally, there is a section called "For Further Exploration," where you can delve even deeper and apply the lessons that you learn from each chapter to your professional and personal life. The five "*E's*" in this exploratory section (example, explanation, exhortation, environment, and experience) are based on concepts of moral education set forth by Professor Kevin Ryan in a 1986 article for the *Phi Delta Kappan*.

By the time you have finished reading *Tough Choices for Teachers*, we know that you will come away with an easy-to-use process for ethical decision making, one that you can implement throughout your entire career. You *can* make great choices that will help you become an exceptional educator. Perhaps even better, you will be able to enact and model this design for good decision making with the young people whom you interact with every day!

~

Acknowledgments

Bob would like to give thanks to his family members, who have endured his multifaceted career opportunities. Ginger, my wife of forty-six years and friend for sixty-five years, has been the mainstay of the family, even as she pursued her own career as a religious educator. Our children, Dr. Bob Jr., Susan, Deborah, Karen, Amy, and Paul, have provided me with many of the stories told in my classes about public and private education from the 1960s through today. That five of the children became educators is remarkable.

Also to be recognized are my inspirational high school English teacher, Rev. Robert Barth, SJ, and my advisor and mentor at the University of Buffalo, Dr. Charles Cooper, who taught me how to write and to survive as a professor. To my deans at the University of San Diego, Dr. William Elliott, Dr. Edward De Roche, and Dr. Paula Cordeiro, know how much your support and direction have meant to this transplanted Easterner.

Special thanks go to my colleague and friend Professor Larry Hinman, who brilliantly presented ethical theories to our joint classes of undergraduates. We were indeed good teammates. To my latest teammate, Dr. Rebecca Wilke, it has been a joy to collaborate with you on this text. Your knowledge, persistence, and patience amaze me.

To the many students in my many classes, from the 1964 ninth graders to the 2008 doctoral students, know that you are the reason for doing what I do. I appreciate your patience, your hard work, and your kindnesses. Thanks also to the many teachers from whom I have learned and whom I have taught for forty-three years. I am especially grateful to the teachers from the San Diego

Area Writing Project and from the California Association of Teachers of English and its local affiliate, the Greater San Diego Council, for providing inspiration and good colleagueship during our many years together.

May you all be blessed with long and fruitful lives and with careers as rewarding as mine has been.

Rebecca would like to thank Tom Koerner at Rowman & Littlefield Publishers. His support has been invaluable, and his encouragement allowed an idea to blossom into this book for today's educators. In addition, my deepest gratitude goes to my coauthor, Dr. Robert Infantino. Bob interviewed me for an opening at the University of San Diego over a decade ago. I knew from that initial meeting that I had met someone special, but these years spent as colleagues and friends have confirmed why so many people treasure his presence in their lives. Thank you, Bob, for believing in me then . . . and now!

Speaking of mentors, my journey through life has been filled with so many marvelous educators. May I start at the very beginning with Mrs. Nisbet and Ms. Johnson, in kindergarten and first grade. They opened my eyes to the joy of learning and gave me my first glimpse of the difference one person can make in the life of another. When I finally reached the doctoral program at the University of Southern California, I met two more exceptional individuals, Dr. Robert Rueda and Dr. Stuart Gothold. From them I continue to learn the importance of leadership and integrity in a world that needs more of both.

Often taken for granted are the family members who put up with long hours of typing and even longer discussions about everything from chapter titles to characters in case studies. Thank you, Dr. Steve Wilke, for encouraging me not only in my writing but also in my professional and personal endeavors for almost three decades. To Ryan and Jared, you have been the best of sons—as well as the greatest built-in computer experts anyone could ask for! Ryan, thanks too for your keen eye and for editing this book in record time!

Finally, words cannot adequately express the appreciation we both have for Dr. Mark Baldwin of California State University, San Marcos, Dr. Stuart Gothold of the University of Southern California, and Dr. Ed De Roche and Dr. Larry Hinman of the University of San Diego for their insights and expertise. Their combined efforts truly have added those finishing touches that most authors only dream about attaining. Many blessing to each one of you!

~

A Note to the Reader

Since this book has been designed specifically for you, we wanted to start with some information on how best to use the pages that follow. We hope that these case studies will encourage you to look at the educational opportunities ahead of you with great anticipation and excitement—and certainly not with any fear of the unexpected. Teaching is an amazing profession, one that truly does impact lives on a daily basis and one that will make a difference to the future of humankind.

That being said, we would be remiss not to include warning signs for problems and pitfalls that you might face in the future. Many of these educational dilemmas involve relationships because this is such a people-oriented profession. Our interactions with others can be some of the most important, meaningful, and even joyful aspects of living. But, as you've no doubt already experienced, they can be some of the most difficult and challenging as well. Several of the chapters in *Tough Choices for Teachers* deal with the problems involved in student/adult or adult/adult relationships.

Other case studies discuss the realities of the workplace environment. For instance, how can you best handle issues about school property or deal with pressures about grading? Still other scenarios help you think about topics like honesty and integrity, allowing you to analyze what you believe and value in unique, proactive ways.

As you begin each chapter, we encourage you to reflect on your own experiences with the key issue covered by the case. What in your background has caused you to believe as you do? How have society, culture, family, and even faith impacted the way you make choices and decisions? In addition, we urge you to delve deeply into the questions that follow each case study. What would you really do if you were in the shoes of the people involved?

We highly recommend that you use a journal to record many of these thoughts as you read the book. Journaling is simply writing down ideas in a notebook so that you can process those thoughts at the time as well as look back on them in the days that follow. We ask reflective questions of you throughout the book, but many of the case studies themselves may evoke some strong feelings or emotions on your part that you will want to put down on paper.

For those of you in teaching positions, you may have already experienced some of these ethical dilemmas during your time in the classroom. Perhaps a few of you are even contemplating whether to seek tenure and remain in the teaching profession based on some of the "tough choices" you have already had to make. You are not alone in these feelings, but we encourage you to weigh your current frustrations with the benefits of working in a field where your true passion lies. Take time to reflect on the problems that you have encountered. Then see how the skill sets offered in this book may empower your future decision making and relieve your frustrations.

Finally, as you will quickly discover, many of the scenarios in this book— just like those in real life—have multiple solutions. While the notion that everything should have "one right answer" sounds appealing, this is not usually the case. Depending upon the circumstances, people involved, and even time constraints, certain decisions will need to be made for the educational process to continue. *Tough Choices for Teachers* is designed to help you hone your decision-making skills and learn the process of thinking ethically about issues in this profession. So, as you work through each case study in the upcoming chapters, you will have an opportunity to consider many possible solutions from varying perspectives.

We have included reference citations within in the text that you can find in the References section at the end of the book. Appendixes B and C also list source material about ethics and values, as well as some books that we have found helpful in our careers and in the classes that we have taught.

It is our desire that *Tough Choices for Teachers* will make the path of your educational journey much smoother, safer, and more successful. You have selected a profession that is profoundly complex, yet ripe with opportunities to impact the world around you quite powerfully. Enter teaching with your eyes wide open, encouraged by the knowledge that the wise and ethical choices you make *can* and *will* make a difference in your life and in the lives of others.

~

A Note to the Instructor

As professors in the field of education, we know that you have many materials from which to choose. So, in addition to offering you our deepest gratitude, we also hope to share some hints about how you might best use this book. We have had the opportunity to present case studies to numerous groups over the years, and we have often found that they are not only well received but also highly effective in promoting the process of ethical inquiry. Many readers can already relate to some of the "sticky" situations our characters find themselves in; others are stunned to discover that some educators can act so unprofessionally. With such a range of possible reactions, we urge you, first and foremost, to be prepared for many types of responses to the issues in these cases.

Before you assign the case study reading, you may want to spend some time discussing the key issue at hand in each chapter with your students. For example, honesty is the value that lies at the heart of the first case, "The Truth and Its Consequences." You may want to start a conversation in class concerning the students' thoughts about honesty, beginning with questions like, Is it always best to tell the truth? Are there ever situations in which it's okay to lie? Help your students process the "whys" of what they believe. Is their stance on honesty about personal choices, or has it been impacted by other influences in their lives? What might those influences be?

We have found that adding a journaling component as students read this book can be very beneficial. Students can write down their thoughts on some of the key ethical concepts as they are reading the text, and they will have many memories and ideas to share when they come to class. We give them prompts throughout the text to put some of their thoughts down in a journal, but they may need some assistance from you to get started—especially those who have not done much journaling in the past.

At the end of each case study chapter, we have included a section entitled "Questions for Consideration." The students' responses to these questions become excellent discussion opportunities for your classroom. You may choose to break students into smaller groups in order to facilitate this discussion time better. Then, someone from each group can share findings—perhaps answers that the participants had in common or about which they disagreed.

We also encourage you to help students work through the follow-up section entitled "For Further Exploration." In particular, some students will need ideas about how they can apply what they have learned to their own classrooms now and in the future. How can these teachers assist their own students in developing the values that they will need to make good decisions about future ethical choices?

Further, we have included a case study/role-play as appendix A, "Helping Student Athletes or Helping Students with Special Needs: An Ethical Dilemma." This detailed scenario will allow you to put a case into practice within your classroom setting. This appendix will provide more explanation, but suffice it to say that you can have your students assume roles based on a real-life ethical situation, one faced in many communities: how best to spend limited resources. We recommend utilizing this applied approach as students wrap up their reading so that they will have sound processing skills when they play various roles in the scenario.

Finally, we offer a list of resources for your students' additional reading and further research. This is only an introductory list, and we encourage students to share new material with you and with each other. However you choose to implement *Tough Choices for Teachers*, we wish you and your students great success as you journey through these critical ethical issues in education today.

CHAPTER ONE

~

Thinking about Ethics

It appears to me that in Ethics, as in all other philosophical studies, the difficulties and disagreements, of which history is full, are mainly due to a very simple cause: namely to the attempt to answer questions, without first discovering precisely what question it is which you desire to answer.

—George Edward Moore, *Principia Ethica*
(originally published in 1903)

If you surveyed people on the street and asked them if ethics were important to them, no doubt many of them would respond not only affirmatively but with an emphatic yes. If you then asked these same individuals to define their concept of the subject of ethics or to explain their own system of ethical inquiry, the conversation might come to a complete standstill. This is not because citizens of the twenty-first century are ignorant about ethics but rather because the process of making decisions in modern society has become extremely complex. And, as the philosopher George Moore so eloquently puts it in the quote above, such complexity has existed throughout human history.

The ancient Greeks became some of the first philosophers to attempt to analyze and define the concept of ethics. Their word *ethos*, which literally means "character," helped define what we now explain as "the system or code of morals of a particular person, religion, group, profession, etc." Ethics can also be explained as "the study of standards of conduct and moral judgment; moral philosophy" (Agnes and Guralnik 2007). If, indeed, the very nature of

1

ethical thinking depends on a group of people in a certain place at a specific time, then the concept would seem to be always in flux. After all, people change, circumstances change, and times definitely change.

It is no wonder that the average person has such a difficult time defining the term *ethics*, let alone his or her own process of ethical decision making. Most of us would agree that morals and values are essential guidelines for healthy, happy living. We admire people of good character and strive to be so esteemed by our family members, friends, and colleagues. If we surveyed those same people on the street and asked them whether honesty and integrity were values they would strive for in their own lives, as well as ones they hoped others around them would exhibit, undoubtedly we would once again receive resoundingly affirmative answers.

The same would no doubt be true of other character qualities valued by many societies around the world. Think about ideals like courtesy, respect, responsibility, and commitment. Don't you want to incorporate these into your life? Aren't these also qualities that we would hope to see in the next generation of citizens? And, as educators, do we not strive to teach these principles and model them within our classrooms?

You have probably read about the emphasis on character education in school curriculums throughout the United States. In one compilation of various programs, De Roche and Williams (2001) noted that specific character qualities appear repeatedly as basic core values that are highly regarded by educators, parents, and community members alike—ones they feel must be passed on to young people as they move through the educational process.

A Phi Delta Kappa study (Frymier et al. 1995) of educators and noneducators across the country resulted in a list of basic skills that should be taught in schools. These included character development and motivational, intellectual, psychological, social, health, vocational, aesthetic, and physical skills. Interestingly enough, a person of character was defined as "the educated person who is honest, responsible, dependable, loyal, and a person of integrity" (Frymier et al. 1995, 29). You can find additional ideas about effective schoolwide character-education programs at the website of the Character Education Partnership (www.character.org).

The concern about improving ethical decision making is evident throughout society, in communities, businesses, and families. In addition to wanting such values taught at home, members of society feel strongly that there must be *an intentional effort in schools* to cover concepts related to ethics, morals, and values. Interestingly, Kidder (2003) points out that having a strong affinity to sound values doesn't necessarily make solving the tough choices in life any easier, though it will certainly be beneficial in the decision-making process. Also, the teaching of the topics listed above does not simply involve developing a specific curriculum and implementing it at some point during the school year. Students learn best by seeing concepts continually, especially when the values are routinely exhibited by mentors whom they respect.

In *The Death of Character: Moral Education in an Age without Good or Evil* (2000), James Hunter asks an important question: "After all our effort to make a good society, what are the consequences of our actions—intended or unintended—for individuals and communities alike?" (7). As professionals in the field of education, we must ask that of ourselves as well. What are the consequences of our own actions—intended or unintended—especially when it comes to passing on those standards of character that will be essential for the next generation of citizens? How are we attending to the social and emotional development of our students? Are we willing to take the time necessary to understand what ethical decision making is all about so that we can not only make good choices ourselves but also help our students learn how to do so on their own?

Sound decision-making skills are the essence of the ethical process. When a question arises about what action should be taken or how a matter might be resolved in the most satisfactory way, educators have the option to make intentional choices—or not. And the ethical process is not always about what is absolutely right or wrong but rather how we arrive at answers to these types of questions. Are you willing to address these types of problems and questions when they occur and then actually implement your best decision-making skills in order to solve them?

We ask you this now, at the beginning of our journey into the topic of tough choices, because you will surely encounter many ethical dilemmas during your career. How do we know? Because we have been there, done that. In fact, we are still there . . . and doing that! Each and every day we are asked in our professional lives (not to mention our personal ones) to take a stand for some moral value, to make a decision and then act accordingly.

For instance, what should we do when it is suggested that we withhold information on a report? How should we respond when confronted by an unhappy student or parent? A dishonest colleague? An overzealous administrator? Will we be able to tell these people the truth—to stand up for what we believe in—and hold our position? Can our yes mean *yes*, and our no mean *no*?

It's that simple—and that difficult!

You may be thinking to yourself, Oh, it's not that tough to make the right choice. I do it all the time! Yes, that's what we hope, because no one wants people entering the field of education who don't try to make the best choices when it comes to resolving ethical issues or who don't understand why doing so is critical for themselves as well as for the students in their care. Yet, you might be surprised if we told you how few teachers are as prepared as they should be for the dilemmas they often face in this complex profession. Unfortunately, some of the worst evidence of this has been splashed across newspapers throughout the country and has headlined the Internet, cable, and network news reports, especially regarding sexually inappropriate conduct between teachers and their students.

Thankfully, many of the dilemmas educators face on a daily basis do not involve that degree of ethical intensity. Instead, the problems often involve the small choices, perhaps about seemingly insignificant issues, that impact many professions around the globe. For example, how do you appropriately manage the materials and monies entrusted to you by the public? Is it really important to follow every rule in the employee manual? What if someone asks you to "stretch" just one, or maybe two, or maybe even three of these rules? Why shouldn't you be able to put your name on a project without crediting your coworker? After all, she didn't do much of the work anyway.

Sometimes these issues simply sneak up on us, like the angry parent who calls and wants a grade changed—and insists that if it's not done now, the principal will be called. How should you respond to that parent? What will you do?

That brings us back to the foundational concept of this book on tough choices. Knowing what kinds of ethical questions might arise during your school day will allow you to process some of these potential problems ahead of time. It will also enable you to step back when an ethical concern is raised and say something to yourself like, "Oh, here is one of those tough choices I've heard about. What's at the heart of this issue, and how should I proceed so that I can make the best possible decision for all the stakeholders involved?" Once you take those few moments to realize that there is more to the problem than meets the eye, then you're ready to move to the next level of ethical decision making.

Beginning to Think Ethically: Points to Ponder

As George Moore points out in *Principia Ethica* (1998), once you can identify what question needs to be answered, then you have taken the first critical step in the process of ethical inquiry. The next steps you will need to take are equally important. In fact, as you begin to read each case study, you should ask some key questions about the dilemmas the characters involved are facing. Let's call these questions "Points to Ponder":

- Who are the people involved in this scenario?
- What main choices must be made?
- How might previous experiences, history, or culture influence the decision-making process?
- What role does gender or culture play in this situation?
- Why is it necessary to weigh the long-term effects of the decision to be made?
- Would this action always be the right thing to do? If not, why would it change?
- How have you addressed this type of problem in the past? Was your response the best way to handle the problem, or could you do some things differently to improve your decision-making process?

The "Points to Ponder" can be summed up with three main concepts, which we simply call the "3 S's": stakeholders, similar scenarios, and self-application:

- *Stakeholders:* In addition to the individuals directly involved in the dilemma, who else might be impacted by the actions taken (or not taken)? Just like a pebble tossed into the proverbial pond, most decisions we make have ramifications that spread beyond the immediate circumstances. How might this be true in each scenario you encounter—not only in this book but also in real life?
- *Similar scenarios:* Think about situations you may have found yourself in that are similar to the one you are currently addressing. Similar scenarios may include situations from your previous or current educational experiences, from jobs that you have held, or even from tales told to you by other people.
- *Self-application:* As you look at each and every scenario you encounter as an educator, try to apply it to your own life. Whether it is a story you are reading (like the case studies in this book), a problem another professional is facing, or even a dilemma that you are currently dealing with, try to make it as personal as possible. What do you think is the best outcome for yourself—as well as for everyone else involved? What changes could you make in your decision-making process now that may help you down the road as you encounter other ethical dilemmas?

You will see reminders about these "Points to Ponder" and the "3 S's" throughout the text. At these points, we would like you to pause and spend some time considering a particular aspect of ethical decision making before you delve any deeper into the material. You may also want to add some thoughts in your journal or notebook as well.

You are now armed with two of the most important strategies for resolving the tough choices you will face as an educator: *recognizing that you must answer an ethical question* and *taking sufficient time to ask important questions about what is going on behind the scenes of the problem you have just encountered.*

Making ethical choices is indeed a thoughtful process, one that will become less and less time-consuming as you begin to hone your own decision-making skills. And that is exactly what the next chapter is designed to help you do. Do you know the reasons behind important decisions you make in your life? What key principles guide you when you must make a tough choice? Perhaps most importantly, what methods do you want to use so that you can always make the best decisions possible in all areas of your life?

Let's move on to the next chapter and see how we can help you define and refine these critical components to becoming an exceptional educator.

CHAPTER TWO

~

Approaches to
Ethical Decision Making

Shall I show you the sinews of a philosopher? "What sinews are those?"—A will undisappointed; evils avoided; powers daily exercised; careful resolutions; unerring decisions.

—Epictetus, *Discourses* (recorded by Arrian c. AD 108)

As students training to become teachers begin to work in classrooms, and as teachers new to the profession engage students on a daily basis, both groups come to understand that the educational process entails more than imparting new knowledge to their pupils. Teaching is a complex, multidimensional enterprise of human interaction, often ideological in nature, and full of daily decision-making opportunities and challenges. Among the myriad of decisions that teachers routinely make, some involve choices that are not always clear cut and are often unpleasant since they will inevitably result in pleasing someone and displeasing someone else, or sometimes displeasing many people all at the same time!

The problem for most of us is that decision making in general is not always an easy process. As Epictetus pointed out in the second century, it really requires regular effort and exercise. Much as going to the gym is part of building physical muscles, so, too, will intentionally working on understanding and incorporating sound practices lead to greater success when it comes to making good decisions in our personal and professional lives. That's why we believe this chapter will be quite helpful to you, although you may have to exercise your brain a bit to work through the various approaches available to you (as you will see, you are probably already putting some of them into practice).

Making good choices in life is rarely an off-the-cuff, spontaneous experience, although it sometimes seems that way. Decision-making processes develop over a person's lifetime and are often affected by past experiences, exposure to classes and theoretical positions, familial and cultural influences, and previous opportunities to face similar situations. Since we presume that most of you are novices at the teaching business, perhaps you have not had the opportunity to face or make such decisions in the past. Our goal is to guide you through many scenarios that will incorporate the practical application of the approaches to ethics discussed below.

Of course, simulations and cases studies rarely provide the same kind of reality that actual encounters with children and adults do. However, having the opportunity to examine your own principles in advance of, or simultaneously with, actual encounters should prove valuable to you. We hope that each of you has had a formal course in ethics during your undergraduate or graduate education. If not, such a course would be a valuable addition to your continued education. The concepts offered here are capsules of longer treatments found in most beginning ethics courses and books. You can also consult appendix B, "Recommended Readings for Educators about Ethics and Values," for sources that you might want to read in the future.

The principles presented here also focus on issues involving education rather than more traditional ethical discussions revolving around medical or business practices, although there are certainly crossover themes between various professions. The ethical concepts are integrated to give you an understanding of how to make good choices as well as to help you clarify why people sometimes make decisions that seem out of the ordinary. *So, we look at ethical approaches and decisions themselves, since these two elements cannot be separated completely.* There are few "right" answers in the cases presented here. Some answers are better than others, and we leave it to you, the reader, to find ways to make the best choices given the information you have and using the decision-making processes that we present.

Ethical decision making in itself sounds like it should be somewhat straightforward. Here, however, is the problem for most of us: what exactly is *the best* solution to an ethical dilemma? The difficulty with the best-solution approach occurs when two or more people face the same problem and come up with different, often radically different, solutions. Some ethicists refer to that conundrum as *competing claims*, or different and seemingly equal outcomes arrived at by two or more equally reasonable people facing the same claim on their time, money, actions, and so on. How does that happen?

In the next section, we begin to examine how such an outcome can occur by looking at how philosophers and others describe people's ethical decision-making processes. We also look at influences such as religion and culture that impact decision making. This discussion is meant to provide a glimpse of, not a treatise on, ethics. You should refer to this chapter as you write your reflections and resolve the problems presented in the cases. You might eventually discover that you fall into one predominant mode of ethical thinking, and you might also discern what most influences your own ethical thinking processes. You should also be able to identify the processes others use to reach their decisions and understand why conflicts occur.

The Role of Religion and Belief Systems

It is no secret that in a country like the United States, people come from a variety of religious backgrounds. Unlike in many countries where one religion predominates, the United States comprises people, including teachers and students, who worship God from a variety of perspectives, or who choose not to believe or worship at all. These diverse traditions and belief systems often lead people to reach very different conclusions about what their particular God wants or commands.

We are not suggesting that religion or religious belief systems have no influence over, or importance in, the decisions you make since many men and women have strong beliefs in listening to God speak to them. One expression, "What would Jesus do?" (WWJD?), exemplifies a kind of decision-making step that many, including young people, take when they face ethical decisions. Another manifestation is the expression "God (or Allah) wills it." Additionally, statements like "My church teaches . . . " or "It says in the Bible . . . " imply that the speaker's decisions are rooted in a particular religious tradition, or at least that person's interpretation of that tradition. Of course, the problem is that when one belief system clashes with another or with the beliefs of those individuals who hold to no religious tradition, there is little guidance over the important decisions being made. The stronger the belief system, and the stronger people's convictions about the rightness of their God, the more difficult it is to resolve competing claims or to reach decisions that might be better if some tolerance for the beliefs of others were taken into account.

Religious traditions often do not speak to many of the daily decisions that teachers face. Surely it would be good for a teacher to pause and reflect, or to pray if he or she is so inclined, before deciding on matters of importance to their students or themselves. But relying *solely* on divine inspiration may not be the most expeditious way to approach the daily decision-making challenges of teaching.

Ethical Relativism and Ethical Egoism

Two related approaches to decision making are *relativism* and *egoism*. Relativism holds that we cannot make a choice that involves others because our decision-making process is different from theirs. Each person is therefore a unique entity and entitled to choose based on his or her background, culture, belief system, and societal upbringing. The uniqueness becomes more readily apparent if the competing claims are from two or more individuals with very different cultures and upbringings. Relativists might say, "When in Rome, do as the Romans do," because when living in a culture, you must follow its beliefs and patterns of behavior.

As the world has become much smaller through travel and technology, we now know much more about each other than ever before. It is good for each of us to examine the beliefs and practices of those who are from other cultural traditions and experiences. But whether we should adopt or adapt to those patterns of behavior is another issue. Right thinking and decision making take more effort than blindly accepting what people do in their particular milieu just because it is "theirs." Taking the stance, "Well, it's all relative, so I'll go along with it," is a weak ethical position that teachers need to avoid carefully. As you examine the cases in the upcoming chapters, you should make note in the scenarios of positions taken by characters that seem to allow for an "anything goes" solution to a problem.

A similar dilemma is presented by the theory known as *ethical egoism*. This approach to decision making maintains that each person should act to promote his or her own self-interest. Although egoism is a traditional ethical approach, it seems to hold some sway within the so-called Me Generation attitude. Egoism resembles the actions of those who have perhaps reached level 4 of the Kohlberg (1981) moral development scale: *Look out for yourself because no one else is going to look out for you.* Although this outlook may at times seem appealing, the philosopher Epictetus might have something to say about the potential evils that could befall a person who deals with life only from an egoistic perspective.

Perhaps the clashes that occur between older and younger teachers stem from either real or perceived decision-making processes resembling egoism—acting in one's own self-interest. Older teachers, including cooperating or master teachers, might see their younger charges or colleagues as less intellectually or morally developed than they are. One would hope that these younger educators are emerging from such ego-centered stages. But decision making in one's own self-interest may have been the prevalent mode that enabled the budding teacher to survive high school and even four or five years of college.

Thus, these younger teachers must be cautious about engaging in selfish, egoistic thinking in which no one else seems to matter when choices have to be made. If you find that you are still struggling with this kind of "survivalist" mentality, try talking to a mentor and begin building strong professional connections that will allow you to start thinking outside of your own personal concerns and more about the needs of those around you. You will soon discover that it is critical not to let ego get in the way when you are engaged in tasks that involve a myriad of other people—the *stakeholders* we mentioned in chapter 1. Watch the ego involvement of characters in the cases and try to identify when self-interest appears to be the dominant decision-making mode.

Utilitarianism

Utilitarianism, often called the *ethics of consequences*, is at least one ethical step up from egoism, even though its goal is to help individuals make moral choices that bring the most pleasure to the most people. Those who follow a utilitarian approach tend to make moral decisions based on positive consequences, in other words, the amount of pleasure versus pain that will result from a choice or the degree of happiness a decision will bring. Further, this position asks us to live our lives by weighing the consequences of all of our actions and always encouraging the development of rules that produce the greatest good for the greatest number in a society.

We see many manifestations of this ethical viewpoint in schools and classrooms. We hear sayings like, "It's for the good of everyone in the class," for you to do what's asked of you, to be kind to your classmates, to keep your hands to yourselves, to respect other people, and so on. These actions bring about the most happiness (especially for the teacher) and thus are deemed ethically correct or desirable.

Utilitarian principles can be viewed in two ways: by examining the consequences of each act or the rules used to guide a society, even a classroom society. To examine an individual act each time implies that a decision maker must take the time to weigh and predict the consequences of that act. Often teachers face situations that provide neither the time nor the ability to predict accurately what might happen if one course of action rather than another is taken. Thus, there is some element of chance as one anticipates the outcomes or consequences of an action.

So-called rule utilitarianism does provide some relief for those who practice the consequentialist approach to moral decision making. It is easy for us
to accept rules and laws that result in positive consequences for those who
follow them and negative consequences for those who do not, especially
when we assume that thoughtful consideration has been given by the rule
makers. Our traffic laws are prime examples, even though every driver questions the enactment of one rule or another.

Not following such prescribed rules often leads to punishment, an aspect of
utilitarianism examined by philosopher John Rawls in *A Theory of Justice:
Original Edition* (2005). He suggests a "punishment fits the crime" approach to
bringing about a good and just society and justifies the practice of punishment
through consequentialist arguments. We often see manifestations of this concept in our schools, where students (and sometime teachers) are punished for
infractions with detention, suspension, expulsion, or dismissal. Teachers need
to know and understand the consequences as they guide themselves and their
students into following whatever rules the school has imposed, whether they
like the rules or not. We shall see as we examine the case studies in the upcoming chapters how the consequentialist ethical decision-making process
plays out in the day-to-day interactions on school campuses, especially as we
look at the consequences of teacher actions or inactions.

The Ethics of Duty

A nonconsequentialist approach to moral decisions making, better known as
the *ethics of duty*, is most often associated with German philosopher Im-
manuel Kant (1724–1804). Hinman (2008, 167) notes that Kant's ethical
theory has three components:

1. An action has moral worth if it is done for the sake of duty.
2. An action is morally correct if its maxim can be willed as a universal
   law.
3. We should treat humanity, whether in ourselves or other people, always as an end in itself and never merely as a means to an end.

These views are posited to help us decide how we, as moral agents, ought
to act in all circumstances regardless of the consequences (thus the name
nonconsequentialism). In other words, *we should act in a certain way because
it is the right thing to do*. The act should be viewed as replicable at all times and
should respect the people involved because they are free, rational, moral

agents with moral worth no matter what their circumstances—for example, their age, their social condition, or their gender.

The first principle of this theory takes into account our *intentions* when we act. We cannot act purely out of self-interest, no matter what pleasure the act may bring to us as individuals. Our decisions and actions must be the right ones done for the right reasons in order to have moral worth.

The second principle above states that what we do in a particular case should be a maxim or guide for ourselves and for others in future similar circumstances. It may be summarized as the "do unto others as you would have them do unto you," or the Golden Rule approach. Would you act in the same way again, or would you have others act in that way if you were on the receiving end of the decision?

The third principle asks, in effect, how you would want to be treated as a human being, not necessarily as a teacher or other person of status, if someone were making a decision about you. Kant suggests that moral acts must dignify the people involved, including the decision makers, by respecting their individual dignity, ability to make free choices, rationality, feelings, and intrinsic value.

The nonconsequentialist approach to ethical decision making appeals to our intellect as we go about our daily lives as teachers. It is a rational approach, sometimes seen as eliminating emotions from the decision-making processes. We are asked to avoid calculating the consequences of our actions and instead to rely on our rationality alone as we act as moral agents.

Can teachers who make hundreds of moral and nonmoral decisions each day really act in the ways described here? Many would hold that we can, especially if we ask the questions proposed by principle two: *would I want to be on the receiving end of the decision I make?*

Utilitarian/consequentialist ethical positions and Kantian/nonconsequentialist ethical positions have been dominant in philosophical debates for many years. They are seemingly at odds with each other, but each has its redeeming features. Hinman (2008) well summarizes the concepts of the consequentialist versus the nonconsequentialist positions:

> If the moral worth of our actions depended on consequences, it would make morality a matter of chance, of luck. Yet in his attempt to insulate moral worth from chance, Kant seems to have gone too far. . . . Consequences do count. It is to Kant's credit that he saw that they were not the only thing that counted, but he failed to provide an adequate account of their full role in the moral life. (189)

The Ethics of Character and Virtue

Much has been said and done over the years about the role of schools as places to help students develop their characters and moral principles along with the knowledge of particular content (De Roche and Williams 2001). Indeed, in the early days of education in America, moral development was seen as central to the mission of schools. One reason that citizens became reluctant to send their children to the newly emerging public schools was their perceived secularization. Some parents, rightly or wrongly, observed that public schools had begun to focus more on subject content and less on their sons' and daughters' moral development.

The moral development of children in public schools has been an on-again, off-again proposition, particularly during the twentieth century. This new twenty-first century has seen a rise in character development programs, especially in elementary and middle schools (Hunter 2000). Student teachers and beginning teachers will often find established character-education programs in place at their schools, and educators are expected to play a part in promoting them.

Developing habits of character (virtues) in the citizenry has deep cultural roots reaching back to the Greek philosopher Aristotle. He posited that a person who possesses strength of character (the virtues) is likely to lead a life that flourishes (if you look ahead to the beginning of chapter 3, you will see a quote from one of Aristotle's famous works about ethics as an example of this philosophy). Thus, one who does not develop and possess these virtues stands less of a chance of human flourishing. Aristotle contended that the person who acts ethically does so out of a personal strength of character rather than simply out of rational decision making based on consequences, deliberation, or intellectualizing about doing the right thing.

Virtuous people develop good habits, have deep-seated feelings like compassion and concern for others, and seek a proper balance in their lives. They exhibit traits of character often included in school-based programs of character education: respect, loyalty, courage, and truthfulness, among others. Because of these traits, such individuals are successful at making sound ethical decisions (Josephson 2002).

As you examine the case studies in the following chapters, we encourage you to try to figure out the right or best course of action for the people in each scenario. Consider what a "person of character" might do in each case. What virtue(s) would the actor have to possess and exhibit to make or carry out a particular decision? Remember that equally valid "competing claims" are almost always at the center of the ethical decision-making process. Yet, *good decision making has to come from good people making those good decisions.*

Contemporary Views:
The Ethics of Gender, Caring, and Diversity

The methods of decision making discussed above have examined what might be called traditional, or perennial, views of ethics. These topics have long been the subject of philosophy classes and courses in the foundations of education. Most of the authors have been learned men (unfortunately, not too many women) who built their theories and conducted observations and research about male subjects.

More recently, writers like Carol Gilligan (1993) and Nel Noddings (1984) have introduced feminine ethical perspectives that have given us "different voices" from which we can expand our understanding of how ethics affect everyday life for everyone, male and female. Other authors have addressed the effects of race and cultural diversity on the ways in which people make ethical choices, as well as why such issues are so critical for modern-day educators to understand (Banks 2005; Boutte 2002).

As educators, it is important for us to be aware of how our own diversity impacts the decisions that we make in both our professional and personal lives. We must also be cognizant of the fact that others around us—be they fellow teachers, staff, parents, and even students—also are influenced by their own diverse backgrounds and experiences as they make day-to-day decisions. All aspects of diversity intertwine to influence the fabric of who we are as individuals, which helps impact how and why we make the choices we make—both good and bad.

Gender

As noted above, many of the classical ethical theories were developed by men and prominently promote manly virtues and reasoning. Courage, loyalty, bravery, and rational decision making are all described in relation to how men conduct themselves, often in wars or in political or leadership situations.

Lawrence Kohlberg (1981) conducted all of his research on the stages of moral development using male subjects. Rational thinking, influenced by age and experience, is the way to move through his six stages toward the highest, that of being a principled, just, respectful person who earns the admiration of others. Few individuals would qualify as having reached this last stage, with most people fitting into the conventional "follow the rules" mentality of stage four.

Carol Gilligan (1993), a student of Kohlberg, studied women's moral reasoning patterns within the Kohlberg model. Unexpectedly, she found that the model did not work as neatly for females as it had for males. She listened to the voices of the women she interviewed about the moral choices facing them. Gilligan noted that the women expressed a caring attitude toward their choices, particularly toward how their decisions affected others who were important in their lives. This concept of care, in contrast to the "manly" themes of justice, rationality, and responsibility of Kohlberg's subjects, did not match well with the six-stage moral scale. Feelings and emotions came into play much more so with women than they did with men.

In Gilligan's stages we find such issues as self-sacrifice, taking care of self as well as others, and accepting responsibility for whatever you do. She made the point that men and women may indeed speak "in different voices" as they develop as people, particularly as they develop as moral agents.

Caring

Nel Noddings has added some depth to the discussion of *an ethic of care* in her writings over the past twenty-five years. She discusses the duality of caring *about* someone or something and caring *for* that person or thing. Noting, like Gilligan, how women's ethical behaviors are most often relational, Noddings (1984) states,

> It is well known that many women—perhaps most women—do not approach moral problems as problems of principle, reasoning, and judgment. . . . If a substantial segment of humankind [i.e., women] approaches moral problems through a consideration of the concrete elements of situations and a regard for themselves as caring, then perhaps an attempt should be made to enlighten the study of morality in this alternative mode. (28)

Noddings (2002) also suggests that character-education programs, often modeled on Aristotle's "manly virtues," may not be enough, especially as such programs seem to focus on indoctrination. Adding a feminine perspective, the ethics of care, to the more traditional virtues approach is essential for the moral development of *both* boys and girls. Without this inclusion in the visible—as well as the hidden—curricula of schools, future generations have less of a chance of reducing violence, building relationships with others, and solving such problems as caring for the sick, the elderly, and the poor.

Both Gilligan and Noddings, among other feminine and feminist scholars, can help you to understand where you, your colleagues, your pupils, and their parents may find common or clashing grounds. Both writers note that it is *more than nature* that operates the differences in the moral behavior of men and women. The nurturing elements of societies, religions, upbringing, and school experiences also form the different patterns of looking at and solving ethical dilemmas. We highly recommend their writing to contemporary teachers seeking to develop themselves as moral agents.

Diversity

The material in Hinman's text (2008) offers opportunities for excellent discussions on living a moral life in a pluralistic society. As teachers, you will interact with students who come from many racial groups, from ethnic groups found within the racial groups, and from families with a variety of cultural beliefs and practices, some quite different from your own. Juggling all of this information has led some educators to say things like, "Well, I don't see color or race; I treat all my students alike." You have probably already realized that such a stance is not actually possible. Each of us is unique, with a distinctive background, culture, and set of experiences. This compilation must be part not only of how we view others around us, including our students, but of how and why we process all elements in our lives.

In fact, an exceptional educator today will view differences as "value-added," with each difference contributing to the good of the whole, yet requiring understanding and, as Hinman (2008) would say, "moral imagination." Since race, ethnicity, and culture are so central to people's identities, their moral and nonmoral actions are wrapped up in that identity.

Adopting an attitude that says only, "This is the way we do things around here"—a mostly male-oriented approach, historically speaking—isn't always going to get the most positive response. You will note this type of attitude in some of the case studies. Moral clashes occur when the students think or say, "But that's not the way I do things—or my family does things." By the way, older students often accompany this type of response with looks of defiance, passive resistance, or even overt misbehavior.

Respecting cultural differences and incorporating cultural awareness into the decisions being made in both professional and personal settings are among the hardest tasks for teachers, especially beginning teachers. Some never quite get it, while others seem to thrive in today's diverse educational environments. Hinman suggests that moral imagination and moral compromise (but not capitulation) are good bases from which to help both our students and ourselves to flourish.

The challenge for you, as a teacher and as an individual, is to learn to live a life of dignity with mutual respect. Remember, however, that as with many things in life, this is a learning process. Learning how to accept different viewpoints, like all good decision making, takes time and develops over an entire career. We hope that you will stay open to varying perspectives as you begin to implement the ideas in the case studies that follow, as well as all along your journey to becoming an exceptional educator in the twenty-first century.

CHAPTER THREE

~

The Truth and Its Consequences

While both (Plato and truth) are dear, piety requires us to honor truth above our friends.

—Aristotle, *Nicomachean Ethics* (c. 350 BC)

Initial Thoughts

When we consider these words penned by Aristotle more than a millennium ago, not only must we stop and think about his message, but we also have to translate it into the modern times in which we live. Aristotle, often thought to be the greatest of the ancient Greek philosophers, obviously valued truth rather highly. In fact, in this treatise on ethics, he appears to honor it more than he honors his friends—including even his closest friend and mentor, Plato, another wise Greek philosopher who trained Aristotle from the age of eighteen at his academy in Athens. Aristotle valued his teacher so much that he stayed at the school until Plato's death in 347 BC, nearly twenty years after his arrival.

To remain at this institution of higher learning for two decades, Aristotle must have enjoyed Plato's company and his teaching considerably. Yet, based on his short statement above, he valued truth even more.

Can you imagine that? Picture for a moment your best friend. This is the person whom you have trusted through good times and bad. No matter what may have happened in life, this friendship has survived—and thrived! When you need someone to talk to, this individual is always ready to listen. He or she is important to you—perhaps loved by you like a family member. You would do almost anything for your friend, just as he or she would undoubtedly do for you.

Yet, can you say, as Aristotle did, that you would actually put *truth* above your friend? Okay, if not above, how about on the same level? Is being honest with others as important to you in life as this caring relationship? Would you be willing to do almost anything to make sure you never told a lie? In good times or bad, could you stand up for what is right and true and honest—no matter what?

If these kinds of questions make you falter for an answer, relax. You are not alone! When speaking to groups of educators across the country, we've discovered such inquiry often leads to further clarifying questions. For example, people will ask, "Well, does that mean telling the truth *every* time?" Or, "What if it could get someone else in trouble? Isn't it okay to be a bit dishonest then?" And, of course, the extreme scenario usually arises at some point: "What if it would save someone's life? I have to lie then, don't I?"

Without spending time on the details, we usually attempt to get the discussion back on point: the statement by Aristotle *should* give us some difficultly, especially in our times. How can we value honesty and truth above everything else when others around us don't feel the same way? What are we supposed to do when society adds quaint little descriptors like "little white" before the word "lie"? In fact, the marketing world is replete with advertisements for how to stretch the truth, bend reality, or simply hide the facts altogether.

As long-term educators, we can certainly tell you that we have seen the value of honesty decrease in our profession over the past few decades—almost as quickly as declining education budgets. Fellow teachers have been quite frank in sharing how they have withheld information from administrators to get things they wanted. (At least they were honest with us about their dishonesty—does that count?) We know of schools that have misrepresented test scores in order to receive more funding; you may have heard about these on the evening news.

Just so you don't think we have placed ourselves on some sort of pedagogic pedestal, we can honestly admit that we too have struggled on the balance beam of truth. It is a fine line to walk, and truthfulness doesn't come any easier once you determine that you want to uphold it. Like a gymnast's balance beam exercise, truth telling takes effort—daily, *intentional*, and, at times, grueling effort! As we embark on this more disciplined, professional, and very personal effort, we must ask ourselves a few questions:

- Why should truthfulness be important to me?
- What benefit(s) will being more honest have in my life?

- Is trying to be more truthful going to be worth the effort?
- What will others think about my increased honesty?
- Am I willing to make some sacrifices in order to integrate this value more fully into my life?
- How will I be able to track my success rate? Do I need some accountability?

We begin the following chapters with these types of initial thoughts about the key issues involved—*honesty* in this case. We would like for you to take some time to think back on your own experiences with truth and honesty. Spend a few minutes reflecting on your past—your childhood and teenage years. What incidents do you recall that may have influenced what you believe today about honesty? How did your family talk about an issue like truth telling? Since we're specifically looking at the field of education, what kinds of scenarios can you remember from your school days about this character quality? Does a particular example stand out in your mind about how truthfulness was either exhibited or not exhibited during your days as a student?

You may be thinking a lot of thoughts right now. Jot some down in your journal or notebook so that you can reflect more on them in the days ahead. Complex topics like these simply cannot be summed up in one short reading, or even in one book for that matter. But as you begin the case study, more ideas and insights will no doubt come to mind. You can take the first vital steps toward processing ethical dilemmas by utilizing what you already know, then adding new ideas as you work through the upcoming pages. Also, be sure to pause and mull over the Points to Ponder below. We hope you learn a few lessons from the characters in the following case study—lessons that you will be able to apply to your own personal and professional interactions. The story is based on a real-life scenario. The key players may resemble people whom you will encounter in the not-too-distant future. But remember, there isn't necessarily one "right answer" to the scenario presented here. As you work through the case, think about different approaches to the dilemma that the teacher, Christine Kaminski, must resolve.

Points to Ponder

Think about the "*3 S's*" we discussed in Chapter 1: ***Stakeholders, Similar Scenarios, and Self-Application***. Who are the main stakeholders in this scenario? Have you ever experienced anything like this situation before? What would you do in a case like this one?

Case 1

Christine Kaminski entered the confines of her classroom early one Monday morning, balancing a steaming cup of coffee in one hand and a briefcase stuffed with graded essays ready to return to her students in the other. She decided to arrive an hour before the school day began to catch up on some paperwork she had left in her inbox over the weekend.

The newly certified social studies teacher relished each and every morning she set foot onto the high school campus. Chris had been substitute teaching ever since she completed her teacher-education program several months earlier. The sudden resignation of the most experienced social studies teacher had left five classes open for Chris, including three senior-level American government courses.

Perhaps what Chris enjoyed most about her job was the students' eagerness to perform well and engage in the various projects she had prepared for them. All but one, Chris thought, as she entered her classroom and switched on the lights. Marcos Rivera had become a challenging student during the last few months. In fact, it was Marcos's request for a letter of recommendation that caught Chris' eye as she put her briefcase on her desk. She stared at it for a few moments, then sat down in her chair, taking a big slurp of coffee.

Chris had been stalling for more time before writing the letter for Marcos. Despite the young man's initial burst of effort at the beginning of the semester, lately he seemed to be suffering from a bad case of "senioritis." Marcos's grade had fallen to a C–, and, even worse, he had been more of a behavior problem than any other student. The way things were going, Marcos might barely make it out of the government class with a D!

"How can I write a letter of recommendation to a college given his current status in my class?" Chris mumbled out loud.

Silence reigned in the quiet classroom. Deep down, Chris knew what she should do: she should be honest in her evaluation and let the college admissions office know how Marcos was truly performing.

But Marcos had begged and pleaded late Friday afternoon before he headed to football practice. "Please, Ms. Kaminski, won't you do me this small favor and write a nice letter about me?" The young athlete insisted that he must have a great letter from Ms. Kaminski to get the football scholarship the college was offering him. "If I don't get that scholarship," Marcos added, "then there would be no way my family could afford for me to go to any college, even a junior college. I can do it, I know I can! And I promise to show you what a good student I can become in your class during these next few weeks."

Chris rubbed her forehead, the memory of Marcos's forlorn face indelibly etched into her mind. Again, doubts started to surface as she considered what to do. On the one hand, she didn't want to keep a promising minority student—although currently an academically troubled one—from going to college. On the other hand, she would be signing her name to the letter, assuring whoever read it on the college side that she, the professional teacher, was providing a truthful evaluation of Marcos and his academic, not to mention behavioral, standing in her course.

To make matters worse, Chris had run this dilemma by another seasoned teacher on campus. Tricia Rutherford had taught English at Westside High for over fifteen years.

"What would you do if you were in my shoes?" Chris asked.

"Oh, Chris," Tricia smiled knowingly from behind a desk piled high with literature books. "You've got so many other things on your plate. Why are you stressing out about one student? Just write the kid a nice letter—you can skip some of the details. After all, Marcos Rivera is one of our star athletes at Westside, and a minority group member to boot. The principal is always happy when our seniors get into good universities and colleges—makes him look good at the district office. That will be one more brownie point for you when he decides whether or not you will stay and eventually get tenure."

"But I'd have to lie because, quite frankly, Marcos may just barely pass my course in American Government. Shouldn't I at least put that in my letter and make it more honest?"

"If you do, you'll probably regret it," Tricia replied. "Either make it all positive and glowing, or don't write it at all. If there's anything bad in the letter, *everyone* will eventually know about it."

Chris could hardly believe what her colleague had suggested. Yet, if that's how an experienced teacher like Tricia felt, maybe that's what other teachers were doing too. Why was Chris getting herself so worked up over one little letter of recommendation?

But what about my own integrity? Chris wondered to herself as she took another sip of the quickly cooling coffee. And what kind of message will I be sending to Marcos—that he can do what he wants, act out in class, and still get my stamp of approval—just so that I look better in the end? I sure won't be helping his moral growth any if I lie!

Chris stared at the request form for a few more minutes then slipped it back into the inbox. As she glanced at the clock, she realized the bell would be ringing soon. She needed to get her briefcase unpacked and the lesson ready for her first-period class. The deadline for Marcos's college letter was still several days away, so perhaps Chris could seek out another coworker for some advice before she finally had to sit down and either write out some kind of response or give the blank form back to Marcos. At this point, however, she wasn't feeling very hopeful that someone else would give her advice much different from Tricia's.

Questions for Consideration

1. Should Chris Kaminski "fib" on her letter of recommendation in order for her student, Marcos, to have a chance at a football scholarship? Why or why not?
2. What might some of the consequences for Chris be if she tells the truth in her letter?
3. Is there a way this teacher could format her letter positively, yet still be truthful in her reporting? Should she do so?
4. How should Chris have responded to Tricia? Should she have confronted Tricia about her lack of professionalism?
5. If Chris Kaminski had been tenured, how might that status impact her decision making?
6. How could issues of culture, ethnicity, gender, or religion play a role in this type of situation? Should they ever impact a teacher's decision-making process?
7. Are other "stakeholders" involved in this scenario? Who else might be impacted by how Ms. Kaminski chooses to write her letter of recommendation—or not to write one at all?

For Further Exploration

Example[1]: When have I experienced a situation similar to this scenario? Have I been tempted to avoid telling the truth because of the potential consequences that might unfold for me or others?

Explanation: How can I best explain the moral and ethical implications of this type of situation to someone else? What advice would I have to offer if a colleague came to me for help with a similar scenario?

Exhortation: How can I share the importance of truthfulness with my students? What can I do to make a difference in how they view telling the truth and its importance in their lives?

---

1. Kevin Ryan set forth the "5 E's" of moral education in an article titled "The New Moral Education," *Phi Delta Kappan* 68(4) (November 1986) 228–33. Used with permission. This template will assist you in further explorations in all of the cases in this book.

Environment: How can I create a classroom that encourages honesty, integrity, and truthfulness? Can I be a role model for these character qualities?

Experience: Does my curriculum offer opportunities to explore the importance of truthfulness? What kinds of activities can I incorporate into my lesson planning that may encourage the students to hold discussions about issues like truth telling?

CHAPTER FOUR

~

Playing by the Rules

Therefore doth heaven divide the state of man in divers functions, setting endeavor in continual motion, to which is fixed, as an aim or butt, obedience: for so work the honeybees, creatures that by a rule in nature teach the act of order to a peopled kingdom.

—William Shakespeare, *King Henry V*, 1598–1599

Initial Thoughts

It's interesting how you can mention the word "rule" to almost any group and receive the same predictable responses. Many will groan; others will roll their eyes. A few might even add, "Yeah, right!" We have certainly seen similar reactions, all the way from primary school students to practicing teachers. These responses, however, seem to be typically human—and they have certainly spanned the entire history of humankind.

Yet, as Shakespeare wrote so many centuries ago, the necessary notions of order and obedience are what allow a "peopled kingdom" to function at peak performance. Even nature itself, the bard reminds us, offers examples of how directives and discipline lead to definitive results. For instance, when honeybees follow the rules of the hive, they are eventually rewarded by sweet success.

Despite our own nature to moan and groan about all of the rules and regulations that impact day-to-day living, most of us in modern society realize the importance of having such policies. Governments could not function without guidelines; states would be in complete disarray without statutes. Whether in a small town or a simple family unit, everything runs more smoothly when proper boundaries are in place.

Think about a typical day in your life. What would it be like if there were no time limitations? In other words, you could go to work when you wanted and leave whenever you felt like it. Sounds great, right? But wait a moment. This situation would be applied to everyone else, too. So, when you went to the gas station, it might or might not be open. The bank tellers might have decided to take the afternoon off, so there'd be no guarantee that you could cash that check. And how about the grocery store or the coffee shop? Well, you'd just have to hope someone was there to help you.

Here we are only talking about one aspect of everyday life. Imagine if everything and everybody in our society operated on a whim. What kind of chaos would we experience on a regular basis?

Yes, most of us would agree that many of the rules, as well as obedience to them, make our world run efficiently. In fact, a school campus is a perfect snapshot of how a set order aids a society in becoming a better place for all humans to coexist. As we have visited school sites across this country—from elementary to middle to high school—we have found that effective educational settings provide clear, understandable rules and guidelines for their students to follow. In addition, these schools also fairly enforce the consequences when any of the rules are broken.

Having rules does not mean that there have to be lists and lists of regulations for the kids to abide by. Many highly successful classrooms and schools have established enough boundary lines for students to feel safe and to know that their educational experience is of utmost importance, without such rules being overbearing or domineering. Often the educators on these campuses have also worked hard to get "buy in" from their students, realizing that if young people understand the benefits of following the established rules, they will indeed be successful.

Think about your own experiences in school. What were some of the rules you had to follow in elementary school? (For some of us, this is thinking *way* back!) What about in middle or high school? How did some of these guidelines increase opportunities for success in academics or extracurricular activities? Were some regulations in your past simply nonsensical—or perhaps even problematic? For the most part, can you look back now and understand why there were so many guidelines to follow during your educational experiences?

Educators themselves can also struggle within these very same settings. Schools today are influenced by many stakeholders, the local governing board being the most recognizable. But state and federal directives must also be followed. In fact, many of these come in the form of educational laws that have been voted into place and must be adhered to at all costs. Additionally, after being hired by a local district, teachers are expected to operate under its directives as well. The school district normally provides each new faculty member with a manual of its rules and regulations, requiring teachers to sign a document confirming that they have read and understood its contents. Plus, each school has its own set of procedures, many established by the current administration at that site, perhaps in collaboration with the teachers and parents.

In other words, a teacher must be aware of a lot of guiding principles in addition to his or her own plan for classroom management and functioning. Although this can be a bit overwhelming, particularly for new educators, there is also a sense of security in knowing that you are working within an orderly system that will allow you to do your job successfully. Yet, just as in the world outside of school, the established rules will at times present difficulties.

The case study below takes place on a middle school campus in a suburb of a large, urban city. The type of pressure that the educator is subjected to here is similar to what many teachers, both new and seasoned, experience in schools across the country. You may find it surprising in this particular scenario that fellow educators are encouraging the young professional to act in an unprofessional manner. Although you probably won't find yourself in a situation quite like this one, we want you to be prepared for any possible scenario in which you may be asked to bend, break, or ignore the rules all together. As you read through this case, consider your own decision-making process when it comes to rules and responsibilities in your role as teacher or educator.

Points to Ponder

Stakeholders: Who are the main parties involved in this situation? Who has the most to lose? Who could be most impacted by the decision that will be made? **Similar Scenarios:** Have you ever excused yourself from a responsibility in order to play? Did you suffer any consequences?

Case 2

The first few weeks at Mountain Meadows Middle School had been full of activity. The 525 new sixth graders had adapted well to the campus environment, and the handful of new teachers on staff had adjusted right along with them. Koby Johnson smiled and waved to several of his seventh grade math students as they passed him in the hallway between class periods. As he watched the energetic groups of middle schoolers from the doorway, he felt gratified that he had taken on this assignment as his first position in the teaching profession.

It wasn't as though he had not had other opportunities. Koby had shown a natural ability for teaching almost from the start of his practicum experiences in the College of Education. Several school districts had interviewed him before he even graduated, and the one closest to the neighborhood he grew up in was particularly persistent in its recruitment. One principal had encouraged Koby to come back and help work with the African American community that he was from—reminding him how having strong male mentors had helped him achieve success.

But Koby decided to accept what some might have considered the cushiest job, one in an upper-middle-class suburb of the city. For Koby, however, this was the position that offered him the greatest personal challenge. He would have to stretch outside his comfort zone by teaching in a new community with mostly Caucasian students and coworkers. So far, it had worked out well, in more ways than one. He liked his students immensely, and he had already begun to get to know and enjoy many of the faculty members.

In fact, next Friday was the first in-service day for the entire staff, and Koby was excited to spend time with his colleagues in various meetings on campus and at the special luncheon provided by the Parent-Teacher Association. The principal was bringing in a speaker noted for his research on multiple intelligences to keynote the teacher workday.

"Koby," said a voice from the other side of the classroom, interrupting these thoughts. He turned to see Susan Blake peeking her head inside the door that joined their rooms.

"Hi, Susan," Koby responded, crossing the classroom to talk with his coworker.

"I know you've got your prep period now, so I don't want to interrupt you. I was just wondering if you're headed down to the cafeteria for lunch today."

"Yes, as a matter of fact I am," Koby replied with a smile. During the past few weeks, Susan had made a regular effort to check in on Koby to see if he needed anything, and she had encouraged him to join many of their colleagues in the math department during the lunch hour so that he would have an opportunity to get to know them better. "I have to stop by my mailbox first, but I'll meet you in the lunchroom as soon as I can."

"All right, I'll save you a spot then."

With that, Susan disappeared back into her room full of math students just as the bell sounded.

Lunch was always noisy but enjoyable. Since Mountain Meadows Middle School had such a large student population, the lunch session had to be divided into three separate shifts of thirty-five minutes each. Koby made a quick stop at his mailbox, found nothing that needed immediate attention, and headed toward the lunchroom. After purchasing a sandwich from the food cart, he slid into the seat Susan had saved for him at the corner table where a group of her longtime coworkers usually gathered. Koby was already starting to realize how taking this break with other adults made his day a much more positive experience.

"So, Koby," Daniel Gallagher began almost as soon as Koby had landed in his chair, "are you going to golf with us next Friday? I heard from someone that you play pretty well."

"Oh," Koby looked at him in surprise. "I don't claim to be an expert, but I did play a lot at the public course when I was in college. It's a great game, and I'd sure like to play more often. So, who's golfing?"

"Sandy and Tim are for sure," Daniel replied, "and, of course, most of the PE department. This has become an annual event!"

"How about you, Susan?" Koby asked after swallowing a bite of his sandwich. "Are you going to be there?"

"No, I've golfed some, but I just can't get the hang of it."

"Well, you can count me in!" Koby responded, looking at Daniel with a grin. "I guess the days are still long enough that we can get in eighteen holes after the meetings Friday."

"Meetings!" Daniel exclaimed. The volume of his reply startled some teachers at a nearby table, causing them to turn and stare. He waved a quick nonverbal apology for his disruption, and they returned to their discussion.

But everyone at Koby's table almost doubled over with laughter, except for Susan, who looked embarrassed by the scene they were making.

"Look, Koby," Daniel said, lowering his voice to a near-whisper. "Hasn't anyone told you yet that the in-services around here are a joke? Some of us in the math department haven't attended a full day of those meetings in years. Talk about a waste of time!"

"Yeah!" Sandy, a lanky PE teacher joined the conversation. "What am I going to do with a bunch of research stuff anyway? I teach kids how to play volleyball and get them ready for the fitness test. Those of us in PE always make a showing at the morning session, but after lunch we have our department meeting at Breakpoint Country Club!"

Evidently Daniel could read the shocked expression on Koby's face.

"Ah, come on Koby. You mean to tell us you've never played hooky before? Look, with as many extra hours as we all put in, it's not like the district is getting cheated or something. Besides, it's *team building* when we're golfing—and the district is into all that stuff. Come on, what do you say? You'll join us, won't you? We need you to finish out the last foursome."

Koby definitely felt put on the spot as six sets of eyes rested on his face for the few moments it took him to reply.

"Ah, let me think about it, okay? I'll get back to you," Koby answered, rather sheepishly.

"RINGGGGGGGGG!" The passing bell for the next period reverberated through the large lunchroom. Saved by the bell, Koby thought as he picked up the remnants of his sandwich and headed back with Susan to their classrooms. He felt very unsettled about the conversation, but before he could gather his thoughts, Susan spoke.

"I'm sorry, Koby. I forgot to warn you about the golf tradition around here. On every in-service day, it's pretty much the same. Most of the staff stays on campus, but there's a group that feels they have the right to take the afternoon off. I'm never pressured because I don't golf."

"What does the principal say about them taking off like that?"

"Oh, Mrs. Hearst has always been pretty lenient with the PE department; you'll see that they get almost everything they want around here. And, to be honest, she'd probably rather be out with them too, so she simply looks the other way."

They had already reached the building that housed their classrooms, and students were beginning to gather at their doorways. Koby looked at Susan in dismay.

"I can't believe it," he said. "I just don't think I can take off like that. I'm a new teacher, after all, and I don't feel comfortable leaving the meeting without permission."

"That's true, Koby, but think it over, would you? Daniel has seniority in the math department, so when it comes time to look at rehiring you, his input will be critical. And believe me, if Mrs. Hearst doesn't have a problem with it, she's bound to be okay with your joining in too."

When the afternoon came to a close, Koby sat down wearily at his desk. He wasn't tired from the day so much as from the heaviness weighing down on him since lunchtime. From childhood, his parents had instilled in him the importance of following the rules as well as living a life of integrity.

Skipping the afternoon sessions that most of his fellow teachers would be attending didn't seem right at all. Yet, Susan's point about fitting in with the math department made him nervous. If he told these colleagues no, would they hold that against him? Would they feel that he thought he was better than they were—some newcomer trying to teach them a lesson about character?

Koby tapped his pencil on the desk for several minutes, staring at the whiteboard as if an answer might magically appear to help him out of this situation. Finally, he grabbed a stack of papers that needed grading, deciding that he had a few days to think things over and, he hoped, come up with the right solution to this predicament.

Questions for Consideration

1. What should Koby do first before he addresses the problem at hand? Is there anyone else he could talk to in order to process his thoughts?
2. How might Koby be able to stick to his principles and still remain in good standing with his colleagues?
3. What do you think about Daniel Gallagher's insistence that the district isn't getting ripped off when some teachers miss the in-service? Why does he bring up the point about all of the extra hours that the teachers put in?
4. How might joining in on this one occasion of golf impact Koby in the future? How do you think other staff members might view him?
5. What other stakeholders are affected when this group of teachers skips out on part of these in-services? What would you say if you were a parent of a student on campus or a taxpayer in the community?
6. What role does Koby's family, culture, or gender play in all of this? Can you relate to any of the pressures that he is facing based on your own experiences?
7. If Koby were tenured, would it make a difference in how he responded to the situation? Should seasoned educators be given more flexibility when it comes to attending school functions?
8. Have you experienced anything like this before? Do you think there are reasonable excuses for missing meetings or other school activities? If so, which ones? Are some excuses better than others? How so?

For Further Exploration

Example: When have I experienced something similar to this predicament? Have I been tempted to skip out on classes or meetings? If so, for what reasons? What made them acceptable? Would I do that again now?

Explanation: How can I best explain my ethical decision making in a situation like this? Would I be able to convince another coworker of why I didn't want to miss important meetings without offending him or her in the process? If others were unhappy, would I still be okay with my decision?

Exhortation: What is the best way to get "buy in" from my students when it comes to following the rules on campus—and in my classroom? Are there things I can do to help them understand the benefits of obeying set guidelines, not only now, but also throughout their lives?

Environment: Do the rules in my classroom seem fair? Do the students understand them fully? Are there ways in which I can include my students in decision making so that they feel part of the process?

Experience: Can I incorporate specific activities in the classroom that will help my students better understand the benefits that rules add to their lives? Can I include examples of other people—past and present—who have made good and bad choices so the kids can understand the consequences of their actions?

CHAPTER FIVE

~

Time Constraints

Never before have we had so little time in which to do so much.

—Franklin Delano Roosevelt, Fireside Chat, February 1942

Initial Thoughts

Some of you may be familiar with the lines of the famous rock ballad "Time Is on My Side." While the rocker who sings that classic tune still keeps on ticking, most of us realize that time is, quite frankly, not always our friend. In fact, we would probably be more willing to take the lines from another crooner's song and try to "put time in a bottle" just so we could keep track of it a little better.

Obviously, President Franklin Roosevelt felt the same way many of us do when it comes to time's elusiveness—and he made his frank statement above in the 1940s! Weren't things supposed to move a lot slower then? There were no fax machines, cell phones, or Internet capabilities! Imagine what this mover and shaker of his times would say about the world that you and I live in each and every day.

From the moment our alarm clocks ring in the morning, most of us in modern society must meet the demands that time places on us. We have schedules to keep. We must also coordinate with other people in our lives. At work we are asked to be on time, make the most of our time, and then "clock out" at the end of our shift. Even our recreational activities must often be "calendared in." We watch television according to the start times of our favorite programs. We meet friends at "happy hour," and, more often than not, we have to make a reservation for the time that we intend to dine out!

Time constraints impact our personal and professional lives, and this is certainly most true in the teaching profession. Every school operates under a carefully prepared schedule as well as a master plan or calendar for the entire year. Bells often announce the beginning and end of the day at elementary school sites, while middle and high schools have sound systems that mark the specific class periods all day long. Educators must learn to adapt to these specific schedules for the good of their students and fellow professionals. For example, if one teacher lets a class out late, this impacts other teachers who are waiting for those students.

Perhaps one of the most challenging aspects for people new to this profession is learning how to balance their constraints. After the school day has ended, many educators still have work to do—papers to grade, lessons to plan, meetings to attend, sports to coach, and so forth. They also have personal lives that include family, friends, and, yes, even outside interests. If teachers don't learn how to manage their workload, they can quickly discover that their personal lives get out of sorts, which eventually impacts their effectiveness at school.

We certainly understand these dilemmas. Even as we write this chapter, we are dealing with deadlines for this book in order to get it published on time. There are doctoral students who need to have regular meetings in order to finish up their dissertations, and a graduation ceremony must be attended at—yikes—7:30 a.m. on a Sunday morning! Who schedules a graduation that early on a Sunday, anyway? Oh well, at least it's just one weekend a year.

We also understand the difficulty of balancing these professional and personal demands. We have memories of our early days of teaching, coming home with piles of paperwork in our arms so we could at least be home with our spouses and children for a few hours before we finished our workload for the day. We spent many weekends with texts and plan books open on the kitchen table as we scurried around fixing meals and doing household chores, then scooted out to attend sporting events while also trying to plan exciting, engaging, and educationally stimulating lessons for our students.

Even as we completed these first few years as new teachers, we quickly discovered that squeezing other important aspects of life—especially fun and recreation—into our jammed-packed days seemed next to impossible. Yet, things as simple as exercise and occasional nights out with family or friends are critical to leading a healthy, joyful life. Once we began to "schedule" a little personal time for ourselves here and there, we actually became better teachers and better human beings!

Think about your life right now? How busy is it, really? If you are finishing your education, you are no doubt in the midst of classes, constantly reading, and completing required projects. Are you also working outside of school, either part or full time? What about family? Friends? How do they impact your day-to-day schedule? Are you finding it challenging to fit in some "me time," let alone get enough sleep so that you don't feel (and even look) like a zombie in the morning?

Our goal is not to depress you here with the reality of living in a time-oriented world. After all, it has always been that way—and it always will be. The great news is that all of us deal with the same twenty-four-hour day. We do hope to get you to take an honest look at how you are currently utilizing that time and, even more importantly, to analyze how healthy your schedule is. If you are out of balance now, the chances are that this pattern will only continue, if not get worse, as you become busier in your educational profession.

You can begin to make some critical changes to your life right now that will have a tremendous impact down the road. It's your choice—and hopefully it's not too tough a choice when you consider the long-term consequences. As you will see in the case study that follows, teachers deal not only with the time constraints of their professions but also with the expectations that students, parents, and even their own colleagues place upon them—not to mention the added pressure when they decide to take extra classes or even complete another degree.

In the scenario below, finding personal and professional balance is going to be a challenge for the main character, Allison Barnett. Try to put yourself in her shoes. What would you do if these demands were placed on you? Indeed, what is the most ethical course to take when there is so much to do in so little time?

Points to Ponder

Similar Scenarios: Have you ever had difficulty managing your time? What about teachers in your past? How did their time management skills impact your educational experiences? *Self-Application:* By what means, electronic or otherwise, do you keep your own schedule up to date?

Case 3

Allison Barnett blinked, then tried to focus on the alarm clock that softly played a tune next to her. Can it possibly be time to get up already? she wondered. It seems like I just fell asleep!

But the clock read 5:45 a.m., so Allison hit the off switch and climbed quietly out of bed so as not wake her husband yet. She padded toward the shower, feeling an unusual sense of drudgery dragging her down.

Well, perhaps it was not so unusual anymore. Allison, a second-year teacher, had been "burning the candle at both ends" for the past six months. Between her full-time job at Rockford Elementary School, her six-year-old daughter, her husband, and the night courses she was taking to get her master's degree in curriculum and instruction, there was little time left over for anything else—including sleep.

But Allison knew the completion of a master's program would move her up to the next pay scale, and with her husband's cutback at work, the family needed the extra income. Fortunately, his reduced schedule allowed him to spend more time with their daughter, so Lily didn't have to attend the after-school day care program anymore—thankfully, since they couldn't really afford that right now either.

Within forty minutes, Allison was on the road, sipping hot tea from a travel mug—her only breakfast since time was so short. I'll grab something healthy at lunch and try to relax a bit then, she thought to herself as she wove through morning traffic. Was it just her imagination, or did the commute seem to be taking longer and longer these days?

When Allison zipped into the faculty parking lot, she was surprised to see it so full already. Usually when she arrived about thirty minutes before the first bell, there was still plenty of parking since many of the senior members of the staff tended to scurry in right before school started. As Allison passed by the principal's secretary on her way to the mailbox room, Mrs. Peterson peered over her computer and said, "You're late."

"Late?" Allison stopped in her tracks, turning toward the secretary in confusion.

"The faculty meeting started fifteen minutes ago. You'd better hurry!" Mrs. Peterson's tone was even snappier than usual.

"Oh, I completely forgot!" Allison replied, too flustered to be upset with Mrs. Peterson's crabbiness. "Yes, I'd better get in there."

Allison rushed to the multipurpose center where Mr. Barson liked to hold the faculty meetings. She slipped into an open seat in the very back but did not go unnoticed by Mr. Barson, who gave her "the look" before he continued reading the latest district memo on the upcoming student testing dates. As Allison jotted a quick note to find out what else she'd missed during the first part of this meeting, she silently chided herself for being late to yet another meeting this month. She'd never been this irresponsible before.

When the meeting adjourned, another sixth-grade teacher, Melinda Sonders, caught up to her in the hall.

"How are you, Allison? You look tired."

"I am, Melinda. This master's degree program at State College is just about killing me. I'm so swamped—and now we've got testing coming up here in a few weeks. I still have two units of science material I need to get through with the kids. How am I going to do it?"

"Well, I'll tell you a secret that I use whenever I'm overwhelmed with my schedule." Melinda lowered her voice and looked around furtively, as if she were about to reveal something that needed security clearance. "You simply need to give your students reading assignments and packets to go along with them. Then you can get your grading done while they plow through all that material. Plus, if you have time left over, you might even get some of your own studies done while they're working!"

Melinda paused outside the faculty women's restroom, grinning at Allison. To her surprise, Allison let out a loud gasp at the end of Melinda's explanation of "the secret."

"What?" Melinda responded, her grin quickly fading away.

Allison wasn't quite sure how to reply. She couldn't believe that a seasoned teacher like Melinda would suggest such a thing! Giving students "busywork" was an indicator of bad teaching in Allison's mind. In fact, she prided herself on the cooperative-learning approach and hands-on experiences that she utilized throughout her science curriculum.

"Well," Allison hesitated, not wanting to offend Melinda by insinuating that she used inappropriate teaching techniques, "I guess—well, I guess I hadn't thought of that."

"You should," Melinda replied flatly. "The district encourages young teachers like you to get more education, but they don't give you any time off to do it. You've got to be smart with your time, Allison, or you'll simply burn out."

At that moment, the bell reverberated throughout the long hallway as if to emphasize Melinda's point.

"Oh, I've got to get to my classroom," Allison said, not realizing how much time had passed. She thought, I can't believe I'm running this late. I won't have time now to look over that astronomy lesson before the kids get settled in!

Several hours later, Allison grabbed a burrito from the cafeteria, but then she had to rush back to her classroom to finish grading a project she'd promised to have ready for her students to take home that day. While she gobbled down her lunch, Nick Washington, the sixth-grade team leader, popped his head in her open doorway.

"Hey, Allison, I'm looking forward to having you help out at the sixth-grade dance Friday night. All of the students are so excited about it. I'll have all the decorating material ready right after school Friday, so I'll see you about 3:30 p.m., okay?"

"Oh, sure—of course, I'll be there Nick. See you then," Allison replied. She had completely forgotten that the dance was this week. "Thankfully, my curriculum class is cancelled this Friday night, or I'd really be in a jam," she whispered quietly to herself as Nick hurried off.

Allison sat down at her desk and looked at her calendar. Sure enough, she had neglected to block out time for the dance. She scribbled herself a note so she wouldn't forget again, then looked over at the lesson plan book that lay open on her desk. She needed to get things organized for tomorrow, including pulling the materials from the storage room for her science lesson on owl pellets. When could she do that? After school was out of the question. Allison had promised Lily that she would go to her dance class since she hadn't had time to do anything with her daughter for several weeks.

Suddenly Melinda's words from earlier that day drifted back to her: "You've got to be smart with your time, Allison."

"Maybe Melinda's right," Allison murmured reluctantly. "Maybe I need to be a bit smarter with my time. I'll just slip out a little earlier today for Lily, and the kids can *read* about the owl pellets in their science books tomorrow instead of doing an exploratory lesson. And I guess I can make up a packet for next week so they can get through those units before the testing begins. After all, I simply can't be expected to do *everything*!"

Questions for Consideration

1. What is Allison's biggest dilemma regarding time?
2. If you could help Allison make a list of priorities in her life right now, what would it look like? Where would work fall? How about her daughter, Lily? Where would you rank her master's degree program?
3. We are all familiar with the phrase "something's got to give." In this scenario, what should that be? Would this always be the choice you would make if you were in Allison's shoes? Why or why not?

4. Do you think Allison should have responded differently to Melinda's suggestion about providing busywork for the students in her care? Have you known teachers who use this approach sometimes (or often)?

5. If you could give Allison some suggestions about how to complete the science units before the testing dates, what would they be? Do you have any ideas about how she could still do some of her labs and other hands-on activities while dealing with the time constraints?

6. Is leaving school early to meet some personal needs acceptable? If so, when? What do you feel is a reasonable ethical stance for doing this?

7. Do you see any signs that Allison might be putting her health at risk? If so, what are they? How could a health risk impact her personally as well as professionally?

8. In what ways are you learning about "life balance" as a working professional? What career guidelines can help you maintain a healthy personal and professional life?

For Further Exploration

Example: Can I recall and share an example of when I might have been in a situation like this one? Have I been so pressed for time that I've tried to cut corners—maybe at the risk of my job or my health?

Explanation: How can I stand up to other colleagues, particularly those with more seniority, and let them know that I feel a behavior is unethical? Are there ways I can do this by sharing more about how *I* feel (using *I* statements like "I believe that this is the best way because . . . ") as opposed to making others feel like they've done something wrong (using *you* statements like "That's a terrible idea that you just shared with me")?

Exhortation: How can I assist my students in becoming better time managers? How will my own personal example help them value time more?

Environment: Are there things I can do within my classroom to encourage better time management? What visual aids (a daily bell schedule, for example) can be used to encourage students to think about and plan the use of their time?

Experience: Can I integrate stories covering time-management topics into the curriculum to initiate discussions about the importance of using time wisely?

~

CHAPTER SIX

Many Are Called, One Is Chosen

For there is no distinction between Jew and Greek; for the same Lord is Lord of all, abounding in riches for all who call upon Him.

—Paul the Apostle, *Letter to the Romans*

Initial Thoughts

It is nearly always the case that getting one's first teaching job is fraught with peril. The perils include deciding whether to apply locally or nationally, whether to accept the first contract offered or wait for a better one, whether to accept a grade level or subject class that you would prefer not to teach, and whether to substitute for a while if no contract is offered at all. The tasks of making your resume look good and conducting yourself in candidate interviews also pose challenges, in terms of nerves and perhaps ethics.

Of course, those on the receiving end of the hiring applications also face challenges, some of which have ethical dimensions. Interview committees, made up of people from the same school but who sometimes bring different viewpoints, face dilemmas of fairness, openness, good listening, legal requirements, and face-saving among other multidimensional issues. When there is only one qualified candidate for the job available, the task is much easier—but such is rarely the case. In fact, when there are many qualified candidates for the one job and numerous individuals from varying backgrounds making the decisions, conflicts often arise unexpectedly.

We have already discussed how difficult it is for each of us alone to sometimes make the best decision. Think about adding two, three, or more people to the process. In addition to the natural conflicts of making the "right choice" for everyone involved, dynamics can arise within groups that reveal deeper underlying issues that must be resolved. Some of these problems will involve personal and professional prejudice.

Prejudice? Perhaps you are aghast that your authors would even consider that any educated American in the twenty-first century could possibly be prejudiced, especially those in the teaching profession. Well, we do. Unfortunately, we are prejudiced, all of us—each and every one of us.

Now, don't close the book just yet. Let us explain. Prejudice involves what the word expresses: *prejudging*. And, quite frankly, not all prejudging is wrong. When someone is running down the street with a knife in his hand, you will most decidedly get out of the way—and rather quickly. Why? Is the man a criminal? Is he homicidal? Maybe—maybe not. But your best decision, the right one at the moment, is to get out of the way—just in case. You have "prejudged" that this is not a good situation, despite the fact that the man might simply be late to his boss's surprise birthday party, and he was supposed to bring the cake knife!

You prejudged him—but that's okay, isn't it? How many other times a day do we make various decisions based on prejudging that might actually be to our benefit and to the benefit of others?

At the same time, you are right in thinking that most prejudice is not good for us or for others, especially the students in our care. Unfortunately, most of us bring with us a whole set of baggage from our past due to our own cultures, family lives, backgrounds, and experiences, which often influence how we think and make decisions on a daily basis. Our goal may be to see no differences among people, as the apostle Paul exhorts in the letter above, written in the early days of the first century. We would probably like to accept others on their merits, not merely looking at outward appearances or basing our judgments on preconceived notions. But how do we get to that point?

Experience, and lots of it!

After a combined six decades of teaching experience, we can certainly attest to the fact that we have caught ourselves making decisions based on things our parents or teachers taught us years ago, sometimes without really thinking through why we still hold on to this or that method of dealing with our own tough choices. Through trial and error, and even through a colleague's occasionally calling us out (usually very professionally), we have both made changes to those previous prejudicial recordings in our memory banks.

How about you? Can you think about situations when you have caught yourself acting toward someone else based simply on a preconceived notion about him or her? When was the last time you were in a situation when someone made a racial joke and no one said anything about it? In fact, maybe everyone laughed (perhaps uncomfortably, perhaps including you). Why didn't anyone speak out? Why is it so hard for us, especially in peer-group settings, to stand up to intolerant individuals or to speak out against racist statements?

This case examines such conflicts among members of a faculty interview committee. Their administrators have charged them with recommending one applicant for a position in the high school English department. A member of the committee, Kelsey Lizdell, is a first-year teacher of social studies who was added to the committee to present a different voice, that of someone who had recently joined the teaching staff and just gone through a similar process when she was hired the previous summer.

As you read and prepare the case for discussion, consider the processes involved in making an ethical recommendation for choosing the one to be hired:

- *The application:* How reliable is the information? Who checks on its accuracy?
- *The interview:* Have the candidates been truthful or guarded, saying only what they think should be heard? Is a one- or two-time meeting enough to gain a good sense of the candidate? What should a committee member do to gain the best insights?
- *The committee meetings:* How does a new teacher fit in with a veteran committee? How outspoken should she or anyone else be on such a committee? What are the pros and cons of speaking your mind? If inappropriate comments arise, who is responsible for stepping in and correcting the situation?
- *The recommendation:* Does it have to be unanimous? If you disagree with the majority, what should you do?

Points to Ponder

Stakeholders: Do you believe that students and schools are enriched or not by interacting with persons different from themselves? Why? **Self-Application:** How do you handle issues of diversity? Do you welcome others into your life who may be from different cultures and backgrounds than your own? How have you dealt with people who have not been accepting of individuals from different backgrounds?

Case 4

Bill Oldby, the English department chair at New Bern High School in Waukewan, Illinois, faced a most challenging situation. He was leading a search committee of five members, including himself, to add the first new teacher to the department in the past ten years. New Bern High School, located in a middle-class suburb of Chicago, is a desirable place to teach and learn, and most teachers don't usually leave the school unless it is absolutely necessary (the last educator to do so had left two years before due to illness). The student body is 85 percent Caucasian and 10 percent African American, with the remaining 5 percent comprising other ethnicities. Bill's department of nineteen teachers had no one with fewer than fourteen years' experience, and all of these staff members were more than thirty-five years old.

The school's principal, Thorny Franklin, charged Bill with forming a committee and conducting a wide search for the right person to replace Pat Beehan, the American literature and Advanced Placement teacher, who was retiring after thirty-six years at New Bern High School. The school board further charged the committee to search wide and to consider carefully the candidacy of underrepresented teachers, since New Bern High's English department members were all Caucasian and mostly female. As Bill gathered his committee, he passed on these recommendations. Louise Reed, Ellen Franklin, Vic Jacumba, and Kelsey Lizdell made up the committee. Kelsey was a first-year social studies teacher who had been placed on the committee by the principal to help bring a young teacher's perspective to this group of veteran English teachers.

"Where are we, Bill?" asked Ellen Franklin, a seasoned teacher and a niece of the principal, early one morning on her way to class. "Is there any hope of making a good choice soon about Pat's replacement?"

"After our meeting next Thursday, we have to make a recommendation to Mr. Franklin, then he'll send the candidate's information to the superintendent," Bill replied. "It's going to be tough choosing among the three finalists since all of them are pretty qualified in some way to join the department."

After having screened more than sixty applicants for the position, the committee had narrowed down the choices during the past month, finally interviewing the three top candidates: Isaac Dian, Andrea Chun-Lopez, and Paul Schiefer. All of the committee members were sent the following profiles of each candidate so they could once again review the backgrounds and strengths that each one could bring to the position.

Isaac Dian

1. *Education:* BA in English from Eastern Illinois University—GPA 3.1.
2. *Student teaching:* student-taught at New Bern High School in Louise Reed's American literature classes; highly rated student teacher; assisted in journalism and yearbook.
3. *Age:* twenty-three years old, just out of college; worked as an English tutor for Sylvan Learning Centers over the past two summers.
4. *Appearance:* dressed well for the interview but wore very casual clothes during student teaching; has a scruffy beard and a diamond earring; African American descent; single.
5. *Philosophy of education:* all students should be held to high standards; students should be well prepared for college entrance in writing and reading; students should not be given too much homework since their outside jobs and activities prevent them from spending time each night on school work; the classics should be the basis for the literature curriculum—modern literature and young adult literature have little place in a college prep curriculum.

Andrea Chun-Lopez

1. *Education:* BA in English, minor in speech communication, from San Francisco State University—GPA 3.87. Graduated magna cum laude.
2. *Student teaching:* student-taught in inner-city San Francisco in a school with a 50 percent Asian population; excellent evaluations; taught world literature and ninth-grade general English classes; coached the speech team to the county championship—team finished third in the statewide competition.
3. *Age:* twenty-four years old. Did her student teaching as a graduate student, spent a year subbing and completing her advanced certification and master's requirements; is writing her thesis on "pupil responses to literature from the 1950s to the 2000s."
4. *Appearance:* very professionally attired during the interview; references commented on her professional demeanor while student-teaching; told the interviewers that she just discovered that she is pregnant; Chinese American descent; married to a man of Mexican American heritage.
5. *Philosophy of education:* all students can learn even the most difficult material if teachers believe they can; multicultural literature is important for all students to read and internalize; college preparation is one important goal for students in English classes, but preparation for life is

even more important; parents often do not know what it is best for their students to study, so teachers have to be expert enough to counter parental objections to the curriculum and assignments; applying to this district because her husband was transferred to a new job in Chicago with IBM.

Paul Schiefer

1. *Education:* BA in English, minor in music from Northwestern University—GPA 3.51; graduated cum laude; attended the Illinois Writing Project during the past summer.
2. *Student teaching:* student-taught in suburban Chicago in a private, religious-based high school; taught American and British literature classes; superb evaluations; helped coach the varsity baseball team to the regional championship; also assisted with the academic decathlon team and gave music lessons to students.
3. *Age:* twenty-seven years old; served four years as an officer in the U.S. Navy after completing ROTC; was an instructor at the naval training center and assisted recruits in obtaining their high school GED requirements; married with one child.
4. *Appearance:* wore his uniform to the interview; commanding appearance, short blond hair, stands six feet two inches, very athletic; talked about his English and Austrian ancestry; came across as a bit stiff to the interviewers.
5. *Philosophy of education:* the most important thing English teachers can do is to teach students to write well; writing would take precedence over literature study, although the two are inseparable; some students simply cannot or will not learn, and teachers have an obligation to the other students not to get bogged down by the reluctant learners; a classic literature curriculum is important but students should read contemporary literature outside of class and do reports on the reading, always practicing their writing skills.

When the search committee gathered in the English workroom the following Thursday, each candidate was discussed in turn. Louise Reed promoted the candidacy of Isaac Dian since she knew him so well. He obviously added a male to the predominately female department (twelve women, six men); he fit the recruitment profile by adding a person of color, and he knew the school, having student-taught there. "He'd be perfect, satisfying everyone's interests, for sure," Louise stated forcefully.

Kelsey Lizdell, the first-year teacher, championed the cause of Andrea Chun-Lopez. She noted that Andrea added some unique perspectives, having trained out of state in a progressive California university and city, and might also take over the speech team from a teacher who was interested in giving it up. Kelsey also pointed out how difficult it was for her to break in as a young faculty member and added, "I would welcome another young female on campus, especially one who has such a wonderful multicultural background in addition to her great resume."

Vic Jacumba insisted that Paul Schiefer was the best candidate. He noted that Paul was more mature, married, had military experience teaching young men and women (much like Vic's own experience), and could coach baseball when the present coach retired in two years. "He'd hit the ground running from day one," Vic added.

Bill Oldby listened as Ellen also added her own positive feelings about Paul. "He'd fit in with us the best," she concluded, without really expressing her rationale for this opinion. As these teachers weighed the merits of the candidates, Bill was struck by the challenging decision that they had in front of them. All three candidates had many positive qualities that could add to this large, busy faculty.

As everyone reviewed the candidate profiles once again, Vic suddenly cleared his throat. "You know, an African American male really would not fit in that well here at New Bern. After all, we have so few students of color, and most don't even graduate. Why not recommend that Isaac go to the inner city to teach students more like himself?"

"Yes," Ellen added promptly, "that's how I feel about Andrea as well. Sure, she's got great credentials, but will the students really be able to relate to her. And what about the parents? You know how they felt about the last ethnic teacher the principal hired for the music department!"

While the others nodded in seeming agreement, Kelsey stiffened in her chair, astonished by what she'd just heard. Could Vic and Ellen truly be speaking for others on the committee—and even for the rest of the staff? Although she was extremely uncomfortable with what had just been said, Kelsey didn't quite know how to respond. What should I say to counter these kinds of prejudicial comments from veteran teachers? she wondered to herself, trying to search for the right response before she spoke to the group.

But Kelsey's thoughts were interrupted when Bill spoke up.

Bill chided Vic and Ellen, though only slightly. "You know our charge—search wide for someone new. We really need to consider all candidates equally, you know."

"Well," Vic added quickly, "we can just tell Mr. Franklin that Andrea is pregnant—and that she will probably be taking an extended leave. Then we'd be right back where we are now, and old Thorny won't like that one bit. As for Isaac, if he was an athlete, I might consider him more. But baseball is big in this town—and that's where Paul will pay off in the end. Let's just play the sports card up with the administration—that should sell them on Paul! What do you say, Kelsey? Wouldn't you like to see more wins for the baseball team down the road?"

Completely speechless, Kelsey hesitated, not quite certain exactly what she should say at this point. The other committee members stared at her eagerly, obviously hoping that she'd agree with them so they could all go home after a long day. Kelsey mulled over a few ideas for a response: Should I really let them know what I'm thinking? If I do, maybe there will be another committee forming soon to find my replacement!

Questions for Consideration

1. How would you answer Kelsey's final question, Should I really let them know what I'm thinking? What virtues or character traits would be evidenced if Kelsey's answer were yes?
2. Vic Jacumba seems to favor Paul because their backgrounds are so similar. Is it possible to get over the "just like us" stance when a committee has to make a hiring decision? What are the ethics involved in doing so?
3. Can you identify some of the utilitarian/consequentialist thinking demonstrated by each of the committee members? What are the strengths and weaknesses of this type of ethical decision making?
4. *Class activity:* With your instructor's permission, divide up into three groups according to the candidate whom you would select during the above hiring process. Share with your group your most important rationale for choosing that candidate over the others. Create a group list of the top five reasons for choosing your candidate. Then try to convince members of the other groups to come over to your point of view. Have those who want to change make both a verbal agreement and a physical move into your group.
5. Take time to reflect on this process, one that you may be facing as a candidate or have perhaps already faced. What does it take to gain consensus on a hiring recommendation? What was your comfort level throughout this decision-making process?

For Further Exploration

Example: Should the ethnic makeup of a teaching staff reflect or broaden the ethnic makeup of the school and community?

Explanation: What does it mean to say that egos play a large role in many decision-making processes, especially those involving the hiring of others?

Exhortation: Kelsey seems to want to exhort her colleagues to become less prejudiced in their thinking. Is it possible for people to leave their cultural baggage behind and get beyond long-held views on race? How do I feel about the possibility of leaving my own views behind?

Environment: What factors in the environment of this school may have contributed to the kind of dialogue happening in the case? What factors in my teaching experiences have affected my school's environment?

Experience: Kelsey's choice here is whether or not to act as a moral agent. Who in my experience has acted as a moral agent worth emulating as I progress in my teaching career?

CHAPTER SEVEN

$\sim$

Property Matters

What a person chooses to do will greatly determine the quality of that person's life.

—Harry and Rosemary Wong, *The First Days of Class: How to Be an Effective Teacher*

Initial Thoughts

Several years ago, we were working with a large school district as it prepared new teachers for service in the schools. The concept was to provide monthly workshops for these nontenured teachers in areas such as multicultural education, classroom management, and communication skills that would help ensure their success during their first few years in the district. During one of our preparation sessions, some of the facilitators got into a debate over whether or not we should spend time discussing issues like morals and values. One presenter piped in her opinion: "We shouldn't have to spend valuable time on those topics; these teachers understand things like common courtesy and respect."

Another facilitator quickly retorted, "There's no such thing as *common* anything anymore."

After mulling over his reply for some time, we finally came to the conclusion that our colleague was probably more right than wrong. As much as we might not want to admit it, many of the values that we *assume* everyone else shares are not quite as commonly held as they were in the past. This even includes a lack of consideration and respect for others' property.

Consider the number of ways you are reminded each day about mere ownership issues. Signs are posted in front of homes that read "private property" (sometimes with the additional emphasis of "keep out"). Many businesses also hang reminders about where you can park in order to obtain their services, and when you enter the business, you may even find their pens attached to cords so no one walks off with them. Schools, hospitals, and churches now stamp their names on property such as chairs, desks, and garbage cans so that people won't take them. Yes, even garbage cans! Can you imagine anyone wanting to steal someone else's refuse collectors?

Sometimes these property matters might seem silly—after all, what is the value of a single pen to a business anyway? But if a pen is taken from the business every day—maybe during every hour of every day—that cost adds up quickly, especially after 365 days each year. And cost is only part of the issue at hand. The real point is that the pen truly belongs to the owners. After all, it is *their* property, and property truly does matter to most people.

Think about a time when you had something taken from you. Perhaps it was something small, so it didn't bother you too much. But maybe it was something of much greater value—like a cell phone, a wallet, or even a car! These events are not merely inconvenient; they are also unsettling and upsetting because they involve a personal violation. Something of *yours* was taken by someone else. They had no right to it, and, to add insult to injury, they had absolutely no concern about how you would feel once the deed was done.

As uncomfortable as it may be, we'd like you to ruminate on those past feelings for a bit. What went through your mind when you discovered your property had been taken? Maybe someone damaged an item of yours. Did you get angry? Were you hurt? How do you feel about the situation now? Does it still bother you? Add some of these thoughts to your journal or notebook so you can process these feelings more as you read through this case study.

Although we realize that most property really is only a "thing," the bottom line is that we humans do attach ourselves to personal possessions. This is partly because we have to work hard for the things we own. We might have spent a great deal of time searching for a particular item before we acquired it; or someone may have given it to us as a gift, so it holds sentimental value as well. Whatever the case, once something is ours, we do indeed attach a tiny part of ourselves to it. Perhaps that's why we are so bothered when the thing goes missing; we lose that little bit of ourselves along with the piece of property.

In addition to all of your own personal possessions, as an educator you will suddenly become responsible for a new set of property. The moment you are assigned a classroom at a school site, it will be filled with property that matters not only to you but also to all of the stakeholders involved in the business of educating young people. The room will contain desks, chairs, whiteboards, storage units, and computers (yes, all carefully stamped with the name of the school). You will be assigned teacher textbooks and materials to use with your students. When you need supplies, you will fill out a request form, and most of those supplies will be given to you, thanks to the generosity of the taxpayers. From pens to paper, scissors to staplers, arithmetic workbooks to rulers, you will be responsible for each and every item within your classroom.

You will also have access to just about everything else on your school campus, too. Whether it's the coffee pot in the faculty room or the Xerox machine in the copy room, you will now get to share the common property of the school site with your colleagues. In a sense, all of us as educators become caretakers of our school community for the seasons that we are there. When we move on—or retire one day—we will pass these items on to the next group of professionals who will take our place.

How you handle this property is also important in another way. Your students will be watching and listening to how you value these possessions. Do you treat the school materials with care—and do you encourage them to do the same? Whether the kids are five or fifteen, they are like little video cameras, recording every nuance of your classroom, including how you respect and treat everything in your care, including them. Speaking of your students, we would like to touch on two rather delicate subjects: socioeconomic status (SES) and cultural background. These are two aspects that significantly influence who we all are as individuals; they don't describe us entirely, but they do help formulate how and why we do things. Some students will find it more difficult than others to understand the importance of respecting other people's property. In other words, depending upon what they have been taught at home and how much (or how little) they actually possess themselves, young people will have different ways of valuing material possessions.

We can certainly relate to these differences. From our "starving student" days to the barely-able-to-pay-the-rent early teaching days, your authors struggled with low incomes and their attempts at high moral standards. We both had cultural influences in our past that might have made it easy to "adopt" property rather than buy it on our own—and our own SES at the time certainly didn't help matters. (For the sake of the privacy of the individuals involved—and space in this book—we won't delve into these memories any further.) Suffice it to say, most of us know what it means to be short at the end of the month from time to time. Some of you no doubt will have had cultural influences such as family, friends, and coworkers who may have caused you occasionally to have fuzzy boundaries when it comes to property matters.

The bottom line is that it seems much easier to have high standards and morals when you have a few extra bucks in your pocket than when you are down to your last quarter. When there have been exceptional examples in our lives of respectful, principled people, values seem to come more naturally. This is quite true of our students, too. So, some of them will need your assistance in learning how to treat school property respectfully, along with the valuable possessions of others around them.

Some of your colleagues may also need help in this area as well. In fact, that is exactly the focus of the scenario that follows. In the case study, we give you a glimpse of a day on an elementary school campus perhaps not unlike one that you'll be assigned to soon. As you read through the predicament of the new teacher, we'd like for you to also think about other situations that you may face in the not-too-distant future, when you may be asked—or tempted—to handle school property inappropriately. What will you do? How will you respond?

In particular, we would like for you to consider carefully how you really feel about other people's property—as in this instance, property that belongs to the community in which you are working. Is a pen only a pen, or does it represent something much larger in the overall scheme of things? As Harry and Rosemary Wong remind us in the quote above, seemingly small choices really do make a difference to who we are and the quality of life that we experience!

Points to Ponder

Stakeholders: Who are the stakeholders involved in these types of property matters? Why do you think they would be concerned about school materials being cared for in the best way possible? ***Similar Scenarios:*** Does taking little things from a rich company make any difference?

Case 5

"I can't believe the copy room is closed again! What is the principal thinking? I need to get this worksheet run off for my class, and I won't have time now because the bell is about to ring!"

Diana Simpson stared at her exasperated coworker, uncertain of how to respond. Tom Kelly looked like he might erupt again if she said anything at all. He finally stormed down the hallway toward the playground where groups of kids were already lining up by their classroom numbers. She looked back at the sign posted on the copy room door and read it again.

Closed until further notice. Ms. Turner will be available from 10 a.m. until 2 p.m., Monday through Friday, to run copies. Dr. Maria Mendez, Principal

Although this was Diana's first year at Hidden Springs Elementary School, she had become quite familiar with Ms. Turner, the part-time staff member who assisted teachers in making copies and laminating materials for their classrooms. Yet, except for a few occasions in September, the teachers usually had access to the copy room before and after school so they could run off their own materials, especially since they sometimes made last-minute changes to their lesson plans, requiring additional papers for the children's work activities.

Diana placed the social studies quiz that she had hoped to copy back in her tote bag, deciding that she could read it aloud to her fifth-grade students. It would take more class time than she wanted to use up, but she'd do the best she could to get through it. *Tom's right—what is the principal thinking? The closure of the copy room is a real pain!* Diana thought to herself as she too moved toward the blacktop to gather her students before heading to the classroom.

Several hours later, Diana discovered exactly what the principal had been thinking. Seated with her fellow teachers at the bimonthly faculty meeting, Diana listened as Dr. Mendez made a few announcements and then proceeded to address the topic that was on everyone's minds.

"I'm well aware that some of you are very unhappy over the copy room situation, so I thought it was time that we talk about the problem directly."

The principal looked over her reading glasses, which sat precariously at the tip of her nose, as she continued. "Someone—someone on the staff—is taking paper from the copy room. And I don't mean just a few handfuls of paper. We are missing reams and reams of paper."

She paused, looking around the room at the more than fifty faces seated before her. Most of them stared back in disbelief, and a few in the back groaned loudly. It didn't take Tom Kelly long to blurt out something from the back of the room.

"You've got to be kidding! You mean to tell us that you've decided to close the copy room up except when Ms. Turner is there because some stacks of paper are missing? Do you know how inconvenient this is for us when we have to run things off at the last minute? My students aren't getting what they need because you're worried about a paper thief?"

"I'm sorry for the inconvenience, Tom, but I thought our paper thief would get the message the last time I closed the room. He or she didn't, and now this problem is hurting our school budget—*your* school budget, to be exact. Paper is expensive, and with the recent budget cuts we've experienced in the district, all of us have to be much more careful with our supplies. What I'm asking each of you to do is to put in your requests for copies to Ms. Turner early. As long as she has them first thing in the morning, she'll place them in your mailbox by the time she leaves that same day."

"How do you know it is a staff member?" Emma Watkins, an older, highly respected teacher, asked incredulously from her usual seat in the front row. "Maybe some kids are getting into that room—and we certainly have lots of parent volunteers around here."

Dr. Mendez took a deep breath and pulled off her reading classes. "I know, Emma. I don't want to think it is one of us either. But we've been tracking the times that the paper is disappearing, and it is usually much before the school day begins. It even happens later in the afternoon when Mr. Allen locks everything up. Almost all the kids and parents are gone by that point. So, the odds are that someone on staff is stealing the paper."

Diana watched as a few teachers shifted uncomfortably in their seats. No one liked the idea that someone at their job site might be taking things that didn't belong to them, especially when it hurt fellow coworkers. Surely no one wanted to have additional restrictions placed on them, but Diana certainly understood why Dr. Mendez had to clamp down. As they left the meeting, the teachers saw that Dr. Mendez had placed a large stack of copy request forms by the door for them to keep in their rooms as a reminder to prepare their materials in advance. Diana took a small stack as she left and headed back to her room to finish up for the day.

"'The Case of the Missing Copy Paper,' huh? Sounds like a short story from a literature book!" Tom snickered as he passed Diana in the corridor. "Who do you think is the guilty party?"

"I don't know," Diana replied. "It's hard to imagine anyone here would do it. Why would they need so much paper, anyway?"

"Oh, who knows? Maybe they are selling it on the side for some extra money. You know teacher salaries only stretch so far!" Tom smiled mischievously as he ducked into the computer lab. Diana continued walking, lost in her thoughts. Why would someone on campus take reams of paper? What could they possibly be doing with it?

The next few weeks seemed to fly by. With parent conferences fast approaching, Diana was busy preparing to meet her students' parents and getting her bulletin boards changed over for the fall season. Late one Thursday afternoon, Diana realized she needed colored markers for an art project she wanted her students to work on the next day. She quickly filled in the appropriate request form, locked her door, and headed toward the supply room, which also served as the office of the school's custodian, Mr. Allen.

As she neared the back of the school where the supply room was located, Diana was relieved to see that the door was open. She thought Mr. Allen might be out securing the buildings and gates by now. Diana looked into the room, expecting to find the custodian, but spotted Emma Watkins instead. Emma turned quickly at the sound of Diana's shoe crunching a dry leaf that had blown inside the small supply room.

"Oh, Diana, it's just you!" Emma's wrinkled face smiled in relief. It was then that Diana noticed Emma's arms loaded with supplies.

"Hi, Emma," Diana said, a bit uneasily. As a new staff member, Diana had reviewed the entire faculty handbook recently—and she knew that no one was supposed to pick up her own supplies. Only the custodian or one of the school secretaries could help you in the supply room. If neither was available, you were supposed to come back at another time. Diana looked out the door, then back at Emma.

"Here, dear, why don't you help me? What was it you needed?"

"Oh, I've got to pick up some colored markers," Diana replied, holding up her request form. Emma grabbed it as she handed Diana a big stack of supplies.

Then Emma did the most surprising thing. She crinkled up Diana's form and tossed it into a nearby trash can. "You won't need that—they'll just take the money out of your measly supply budget. They don't give us half of what they did in the past to spend on the kids, so I just come in here from time to time and help myself. Same with the paper. Copy paper works extremely well for art projects, don't you know!"

Before Diana could reply, Emma thrust the markers from Diana's list to the top of the pile of things Diana was already holding for Emma. The pile included a large package of multicolored construction paper, several boxes of watercolor sets, and two reams of paper. Emma then added a couple of staplers and a few rolls of masking tape onto the top of the pile.

"Let's go, dear . . . follow me with those supplies. We'll divide things up in my classroom, and I can give you some paper if you need it. Quickly, I'm down this hallway."

"Uh, Emma, I'm not sure about this," Diana stammered as the elderly teacher maneuvered past her.

"What's wrong, Diana? You look like you've been busted by Dr. Mendez! I'm not going to tell anyone about this. It'll be our little secret. And, besides, now you know when to sneak down here and get a few things when you need them. It's all for the good of the kids, right?"

Faster than Diana imagined anyone at her age could move, Emma trotted out of the supply room and sped down the hall toward her classroom. Diana remained frozen in the doorway, loaded with the array of supplies Emma had piled into her arms.

"Now what do I do?" Diana's question softly echoed down the empty corridor that Emma had just used as her escape route.

Questions for Consideration

1. What is the best choice for Diana to make at this point? Why do you think this might be the right thing to do?
2. If Diana simply leaves the items Emma gave her on the custodian's desk, what might happen next?
3. Should Diana confront Emma about what she's been doing? If she does, what might happen?
4. Does Dr. Mendez have the right to know about the situation? What might the consequences be if Diana tells her? What if Diana withholds the information and the principal finds out about everything later?
5. What about Emma's rationale that her actions are actually for the good of the kids? How might others feel about her opinion? How may her actions actually be hurting students?
6. What other stakeholders would be concerned about the disappearing items on campus? How are they being hurt by the mishandling of paper and supplies?
7. What other types of property on campus could be mismanaged by staff members? How might employees be encouraged to manage school property better?

For Further Exploration

Example: Have I ever witnessed anything like this in my past job experiences? How did I handle it at the time? Would I do anything differently now? If so, what?

Explanation: How do I truly feel about the property and possessions of others? Do I value school property appropriately—as something that's on loan to me? How would I explain my value system to another coworker?

Exhortation: How can I encourage my students to respect the property of others? Are there discussions that I can hold in class to talk about these issues, particularly in a class with pupils from different socioeconomic and cultural backgrounds?

Environment: What kinds of guidelines will I put in place in my classroom to ensure that the things in my charge are cared for appropriately? Are there ways that I can teach respect and responsibility when it comes to school property as well as the possessions of others?

Experience: How might I let students share experiences they've had with property issues? Can I find time to have students lead discussions about how they feel about respecting property?

CHAPTER EIGHT

~

Credit—and Where It Is Due

He who permits himself to tell a lie once, finds it much easier to do it a second and third time, till at length it becomes habitual. This falsehood of the tongue leads to that of the heart, and in time depraves all its good dispositions.

—Thomas Jefferson, Letter to Peter Carr, August 1785

Initial Thoughts

At this point in the book, you may be thinking things like, There's so much to know about ethical issues and good decision making. How am I going to remember all of this? We certainly understand your concern, especially when you are also a busy, working professional in the fast-moving P–12 school settings of today. So, we'd like to spend a few moments putting your mind at ease.

First and foremost, understanding ethical issues is an essential step toward making good decisions not only in your teaching career but also in your personal life. Once you start "thinking ethically," you will more than likely continue to do so all along life's journey. Second, you have probably noted that many of the *tough choices* in the previous cases have often had common themes: honesty, integrity, responsibility, respect, and equity, for example. In other words, though the names, places, and circumstances may change, many of the basic values and morals that educators should strive to uphold remain the same.

Thus, good decision making is not extremely complex. It does involve some time and effort, as well, of course, as the willingness to process situations through perhaps new ethical perspectives and paradigms. We hope, however, that you are beginning to glimpse the positive effects this process can have on your personal and professional life. Also, please remember that there usually isn't one right way to resolve ethical dilemmas. Many of the scenarios you will face in education can be solved in multiple ways, depending on the stakeholders involved and the other variables—including what you, the professional educator, know and feel is the most ethical decision at the given time. What is important is that you are formulating a specific thinking process to *intentionally* resolve the tough choices that you encounter.

The basic themes discussed in this book are also common in many character-education programs across America—they reflect the same ideals that teachers, schools, families, communities, and business leaders also hope to pass on to the next generation of citizens (De Roche and Williams 2001; Kidder 2003). Many people, including educators, believe that learning to live by a simple code of ethics not only makes us better individuals but also improves our whole society. Choosing not to live by some fundamental tenets, however, will more than likely lead to bad decisions as well as result in bad consequences.

Perhaps this is the crux of what Thomas Jefferson writes about in the section of his letter quoted above. Jefferson explains his perceptions about truth telling, or the lack thereof, to his nephew Peter Carr. The statesman explained that one lie can lead to another, so that eventually the whole heart of a person becomes depraved in time. He warns his nephew that lying eventually results in the loss of all of the heart's "good dispositions" (what we would call character).

According to some historical accounts, Carr was reported to be the real father of Sally Henning's children. You may recall that Henning, who was a slave at Jefferson's Monticello home, personally claimed to have had children by the president—not by Carr (McCullough 2001). Exactly whether Jefferson himself or Peter Carr needed the lesson about honesty more is open for discussion.

At any rate, the third president certainly has had his share of recent critics regarding his character—with many offering their condemnation for his lifting of concepts to include in the Declaration of Independence. Yet, as the Pulitzer Prize–winning author David McCullough (2001) notes, it was not unusual for many early American statesmen to draw "on long familiarity with the seminal works of the English and Scottish writers John Locke, David Hume, Francis Hutcheson, and Henry St. John Bolingbroke, or such English poets as Defoe" (121).

From his prolific private and public documents, it is evident that Thomas Jefferson was quite gifted with pen and paper. However, we must also recognize that people in the eighteenth century did not look down upon the tendency to "borrow readily" (McCullough's term) as much as denizens of the twenty-first century do. Why things have changed over the course of time is a unique study in history itself, but many individuals in modern society prefer to be given credit not only for their published work but also for ideas themselves. Assigning appropriate recognition is highly valued today, and it is also becoming increasingly regulated (if you want one example, see the first few pages of this book to find its copyright explanation).

As educators, we have had to become increasingly sensitive to problems concerning plagiarism. We have instructed students from elementary schools to the university level about the importance of giving appropriate credit to authors whose work they may have used in everything from simple essays to doctoral dissertations. In addition, as writers ourselves, we certainly strive to reference every person's materials, and, of course, we hope that others will do likewise when they quote from our texts!

Yet, like the teacher whom you are going to meet in the case study that follows, we have also had our fair share of "identity theft" in the field of education. By this we mean that others have chosen to take partial or even full credit for some ideas or projects that were ours in conception without bothering to acknowledge us at all. As you can imagine, these scenarios created some truly challenging dilemmas, particularly when we were new to the profession and rather inexperienced about how to handle such situations.

You certainly have had your own experiences regarding the unauthorized use of materials. At this point in your educational career, the concept of giving appropriate credit to sources has no doubt been explained ad nauseam. Think about how this one simple aspect of character may have impacted your own writing experiences.

Perhaps, like the novice educator Brad Edelstein in the following case study, you too have been the victim of "identity theft." Someone took *your* efforts—a project you were working on, your answers on a test, or even an idea of yours—and ran with them as if they were his or her own. How did that make you feel? What did you do about the injustice? What did others do or say, if anything?

As a teacher, you will have many opportunities to encourage your own students to understand the value of one another's work and of those sources they will be utilizing in the educational process. You will be able to teach them to give proper credit to these sources, and, of course, it will be incumbent upon you to set the example yourself.

But, like Brad Edelstein, you may not always witness this type of exemplary behavior in other educators. Instead, you may sometimes feel a bit discouraged by those who simply don't "practice what they preach." As you enter Brad's world for a short while, think about how you might best handle a situation like this one if it should ever happen to you.

Points to Ponder

Stakeholders: Why does it seem that everyone is concerned about plagiarism? *Similar Scenarios:* Have you ever experienced problems with plagiarism? What about someone taking credit for your work or your unique ideas? How did this make you feel? What was done about it?

Case 6

As Brad Edelstein stepped off the train, the usual biting winds of January greeted him at the station platform. He stuffed his gloved hands deeper inside his pockets while clutching his briefcase tightly under his left arm. Following fellow passengers down the stairs, he quickly headed toward the Stratford School a block away.

The old brick edifice was a welcome sight, even though the two-story structure always seemed dwarfed by the multilevel office buildings that bordered each side. Yet, Brad loved this eighty-year-old private school that still served an inner-city population. He was particularly thrilled to be teaching at all, given the continuing dearth of teaching positions in the state. Even though he thought he'd be working in a public school by now, he was actually enjoying the smaller class sizes and individual attention that he could give his students in this educational setting.

After a final gust of wind blasted past him, Brad ducked inside the administration building, then went straight to the coffee pot and poured himself a steaming cup.

"Hey, Brad, how are you doing this morning?" Brad turned to see his friend and colleague, Jake Williams, coming in the doorway with an armload of books.

"Hi," Brad replied. "What have you got there?"

"Oh, I'm going to get my eighth graders started on their new novel. I can't believe it, the second semester just started and I'm already feeling behind. Are you ready to shoot some hoops after school today?"

"You bet!" Brad smiled. He looked forward to Wednesday afternoons when some of the staff got together in the gym for a game of basketball. "I'll see you later, Jake."

Brad grabbed his briefcase, checked his mailbox, then walked down the long indoor corridor toward his classroom. That's when he nearly bumped into Carli Grant.

"Oh, hello, Bradley," Carli exclaimed. "I was hoping to run into you today. I've finished the study hall assignments for next month. Here's a copy of your schedule. Be sure to double-check it with your calendar as quickly as possible. See you later, Bradley."

And as quickly as she'd appeared, Carli vanished around a corner. Unfortunately, the good feelings Brad had been experiencing so far that morning dissipated rapidly. "I guess I'm going to have to deal with this situation sooner or later—I can barely stand to see Carli let alone talk to her. And why on earth does she keep calling me Bradley? I've reminded her at least a dozen times that my name is Brad! She must be doing it to tick me off!" Brad muttered to himself as he continued down the hallway.

Brad didn't need his coffee now; he was plenty steamed. His thoughts raced over the events of the last few months. Carli Grant, the team leader for the junior high social studies department at the Stratford School, had asked him to help her come up with a proposal for a collaborative school–business partnership with a nearby office supply store. At first, Brad had been excited by the opportunity to assist this veteran teacher, especially since this was only his second year at the school. He soon realized, however, that Carli's idea of "teamwork" meant that he would end up doing nearly all of the work.

But that wasn't the worst of it. After many extra hours spent putting the proposal together and several meetings with the office supply store manager, he had turned over the packet to Carli. She summarily put her name—and her name only—on the proposal and turned it into the principal. Brad inadvertently learned that bit of information from Judy, the principal's secretary. Judy had handed the final proposal to Brad the previous week when she learned he was going into a team meeting that Carli would be leading.

"Oh, Brad, could you give this to Ms. Grant when you get to the meeting. Mrs. Takamura is so pleased that the junior high will be getting some wonderful materials thanks to Ms. Grant's efforts."

Brad was speechless, especially when he searched and discovered his name wasn't even in the body of the proposal. He wanted to confront Carli at the meeting, but on the way there, he changed his mind. Making a senior staff member look bad in front of other colleagues wasn't his idea of professionalism. Besides that, he held strongly to his religious traditions that vengeance belonged to a higher authority.

Yet, Brad had been pretty upset at that meeting. Actually, every time he saw Carli, he still felt tremendous anger, an emotion that he didn't like to admit to harboring toward a fellow human being. But he wasn't quite sure how to handle the situation. After all, he didn't want to offend one of the people who would be responsible for renewing his contract—not in this teaching market. What if he simply went straight to the principal and explained things. Would she take his side or Carli's? And if Mrs. Takamura decides not to renew my contract because of this, he wondered, where else could I go right now? There are no other job openings for teachers in the city. Maybe I should simply bite the bullet and keep quiet. His thoughts raced as he tried to figure out the best decision to make.

Brad mulled over the unpleasant situation as he unlocked his classroom and switched on the lights. Glancing at the clock, he realized he only had fifteen minutes to organize a few things before his students arrived for their history lesson. As he grabbed his lesson plan, he decided, I'll worry about Carli later. Maybe I can ask Jake for advice. He's been here several years, so he might have some ideas about what to do.

As the morning went by, Brad taught his history lesson to three different groups of Stratford students. Dressed in their preppy uniforms, these bright, energetic students revived Brad's spirit, and by the time his afternoon classes began, he'd forgotten all about Carli Grant.

About 1:30 p.m., a teacher's assistant from the office came in with a note for Brad. While his students continued to work on a quiz they'd been given, Brad looked over the slip of paper. It was a note from the principal, Mrs. Takamura, asking if he would stop by her office during his prep period the next hour. Now what's happened? She couldn't know that I wanted to talk to her about the proposal, could she? he wondered to himself nervously.

Within the hour, Brad found out exactly what was on the principal's mind.

"Brad, we have a problem," Mrs. Takamura began in her usual no-nonsense manner. "It seems that your student, Alyssa Jones—the one who won the essay contest in November—may have plagiarized some of the contents."

"What!" Brad couldn't help but exclaim. "I can't believe that. Alyssa is a fine student with a creative mind. I simply can't see her ever doing that."

"Nevertheless, Mr. Korkova from the English department was going to use her essay as an example in his courses when he noticed some of the lines looked similar to a novel that he had used last year with the seventh graders. He found several phrases and ideas that Alyssa utilized without quoting her source. I'm afraid we'll have to call a special meeting of the department heads to discuss whether or not we should contact the computer company that ran the contest and let them know we cannot accept the free software programs they awarded the school, even though we certainly could use them. We have high ethical standards here at the Stratford School—especially in such matters as plagiarism!"

Brad nodded, but the words he wanted to say stuck in his throat. He sat motionless in his chair as a few ideas raced through his mind. *If she thinks this is a problem, I wonder what Mrs. Takamura would say if she discovered one of her veteran teachers had not only lifted a few lines but had also actually stolen someone's entire project!*

Mrs. Takamura noticed Brad's hesitation. "Well, what do you have to say, Brad? How are we going to handle this plagiarism problem?"

Questions for Consideration

1. What are some of the most unsettling aspects of Carli Grant's actions? What ethical dilemmas has she created for this new teacher?
2. Although Brad is new to the school, does he still have a responsibility to uphold the school's integrity? What about his own personal ethics? How might these play a part in what he decides to do in this situation?
3. What problems might arise if Brad does decide to speak to the principal about Carli? What could happen if he confronts Carli by himself?
4. If you were Brad's friend Jake, what advice might you offer him? Would you help in an intervention—or would it be better to stay on the sidelines?
5. Do you think things might be different if this scenario happened at a public school instead of a private school? If so, how? Also, how does a current job market impact the decision-making process for Brad?
6. What should happen to the student, Alyssa, and her essay? What first steps should the school take in this scenario? What should the computer company do?
7. How might gender impact Brad's decision-making process? If the gender roles were changed, would a young female teacher feel more or less inclined to confront an older male department head? Why?

For Further Exploration

Example: Have I, or has someone I know, encountered plagiarism? What were the circumstances? How did the dilemma get resolved?

Explanation: Giving proper credit is a big part of what we want to teach children in schools. How can I help clarify the importance of giving credit to others as I teach my regular curriculum?

Exhortation: If my school has character guidelines or a code of ethics, do I know what that entails? How can I encourage my students to follow such guidelines?

Environment: What opportunities will my students have to practice good decision making in my classroom, especially when it comes to plagiarism? What role will my behavior play in the practices of these students?

Experience: Do my assignments encourage students to think openly and freely, or might the students be afraid to be creative and try to "borrow" ideas from someone else in order to please me or to earn a high grade? Do I take the time necessary to show them how to properly quote sources and to give credit in appropriate ways?

~

CHAPTER NINE

Making the Grade

But rewards and punishments, to speak frankly, are the desk of the soul, that is, a means of enslaving a child's spirit, and better suited to provoke than prevent deformities.

—Maria Montessori, *The Discovery of the Child*

Initial Thoughts

Perhaps no other issue in education evokes as much angst as that of grading—angst for the educators, but far more for the recipients of those grades, the students *and* their parents. Some experts argue that grading is the most time-consuming part of a teacher's professional life. In fact, Queen, Burrell, and McManus (2001) state that exact sentiment in *Planning for Instruction: A Year-Long Guide*. Young people perceive grades as the reward for their efforts, whether good or bad.

The subject of assessment is rather elusive. As we reviewed some of our favorite sources of educational materials (a few that are truly seminal works in the field), the topic of grading was, frankly, quite sparsely covered. The material we did discover expressed that grading was a "major concern for teachers" (Jensen and Kiley 2000) and "should always be done in reference to learning criteria" (Wong and Wong 1998). Even Ornstein and Levine's classic *Foundations of Education* (2007) offers a plethora of information on curriculum reforms and new instructional approaches but few specific guidelines on how best to assess these reforms within the day-to-day classroom.

To be fair to these authors, we would add that they truly do cover an enormous amount of material on the vast field of education. It is no easy feat to condense all of that material into a single volume that a normal person can read! Yet, if assessing, grading, and reporting are indeed such important tasks for teachers, shouldn't there be a wide array of helpful information for educators on the subject? Unless you have been fortunate enough to take a specific class on assessment techniques, your knowledge of testing and grading is not very extensive.

Instead, many of us are left on our own to determine how we should establish the best system for assessing our students, and often that means drawing from our past experiences. In other words, we tend to grade our students based on how we were graded when we were in school.

Think about that for a moment. If we have never received formal (or even informal) training on how to set up a grading system that is fair, equitable, clear, concise, explainable, and, most of all, accurate in its reflection of progress attained, then how can we be assured that our method of assessment is of the highest quality for our students?

No wonder so many educators experience angst, to some degree or another, when it comes to grading. Your authors have certainly been on both sides of the report card, so to speak. As students, even as recently as graduate school, we anxiously awaited our grades. In those days they weren't posted on a website or sent electronically; we actually received tangible mail apprising us of our achievement in a particular class. These old-fashioned grade reports, however, were just as painful to open as modern-day e-mails, especially when the grade fell short of what we thought we had earned and deserved!

We have also had to grapple with how to establish an appropriate assessment system for the various grade levels, subject areas, and college courses that we've taught over the years. We, too, have had students who were unhappy with us, and, perhaps even worse, some parents have been angry at us. Like the teacher in the case study that you will read shortly, we have also encountered adults who have tried to bully us into changing grades, even threatening to take the issue to a "higher authority" if we didn't.

Fortunately, as we have shared with you in previous chapters, these volatile scenarios are not very common. But if you can establish a sound system for assessing your students early on, you will tend to experience far fewer problems down the road. In order to avoid these pitfalls, as an exceptional educator it should be your desire to set up a fair and accurate system for evaluating and grading each and every one of your students. Indeed, as Maria Montessori, the amazing educator, physician, and humanitarian, gently reminds us, grades are extremely powerful forces that can either enslave a child's spirit or spur it on to even greater achievements in the future!

In fact, why don't you spend a few minutes thinking about your own experiences with grades. Go as far back as your memory allows. What do you remember?

Can you picture the first reward you received at school—maybe a sticker on your forehead in preschool when you did something great? What about the first test you took? Can you see the mark that was affixed to the top? Did the teacher write any nice comments to you? What were subsequent positive evaluation experiences like as you progressed through the system?

How about some of those "not-so-nice" experiences with assessment? Did you ever receive a grade you considered unfair but that the teacher wouldn't change? Or maybe you did really deserve that bad mark, but the sting of that failure still hurts today. Why? How do you think others feel when they discover they've received a D or an F in a class?

If some of these memories are positive—and we hope there are many—then jot down a few right now in your journal or notebook. When did the memories happen—elementary, middle, or high school? Maybe your college years ended up being your best academically because you finally realized that grades were important for your future success. If you have had some negative feelings surface, then write a few of these down too. Why did something as simple as a grade make you feel so bad? Could you have done anything at the time to improve the situation? How might you use this negative experience to become a better teacher for your students?

Once you delve into the case study below, you will discover that the process of assessing your students often involves many factors, not all of which will be under your total control. Sometimes you will have supportive parents; sometimes you won't. Occasionally an administrator or coworker will make sticking by your grading system trickier than you thought. The best advice we can offer is to begin researching various types of assessment practices for this profession, especially ones that you can utilize in your particular subject area or grade level. We've included a few excellent references to help you get started in appendix C, "Recommended Resources for Today's Teachers." In the meantime, take a look at the scenario below and see what kind of dilemma the teacher, Leticia Granados, faces when it comes to grading an AP biology student.

Points to Ponder

Similar Scenarios: How involved should parents be in the daily academic progress of their children? *Self-Application:* How can you develop a grading system that will not only be fair but also be understood by everyone involved? What can you do ahead of time to avoid challenges to your grading system?

Case 7

Leticia Granados paced the floor at the front of her classroom, the heels of her shoes clicking against the tiled floor. The rhythm of the pacing coincided with the ticking of the wall clock above the white board. She glanced up to check the time—ten minutes until 3 p.m. Matthew's parents should be arriving soon. They were usually quite prompt.

A few unexpected butterflies fluttered through Leticia's stomach. Although she'd been teaching for three years at Ridgecrest High School and had been given tenure last year, she still felt nervous about conducting parent-teacher conferences. Especially with these parents, Leticia thought to herself. So far they have set the record for meetings in my career—at least one a month!

But the school year was nearing an end, so the constant bombardment of questions and concerns from the Montgomery family would be over soon. Ever since school began, Mr. and Mrs. Montgomery had been setting appointments to meet with Leticia in order to check on this or that problem they had with the curriculum. Once they had asked her about her background and experience teaching Advanced Placement courses for biology. And although they never came right out and said it, Leticia had the undeniable feeling that they questioned why a Latina was teaching at their son's school to begin with!

Of course, Leticia knew exactly why. Worthington Union High School District had been under a state mandate to hire "teachers of color" for nearly a decade, and the administration had finally gotten around to it a few years before under the threat of losing some of the state's funding. Leticia's advisor at the School of Education had warned that she might experience some difficulties integrating into this upper-middle-class school district, but she felt she was ready for such a challenge. After all, this was the twenty-first century—and certainly people were more accepting than she was hearing.

"If only that were true," Leticia whispered, sitting down in one of the chairs she had gathered for the conference, straightening the pile of papers she wanted to review with Mr. and Mrs. Montgomery. Indeed, the transition to Ridgecrest High School had been far more difficult than Leticia had anticipated. First, although everyone on the staff seemed accepting and friendly, few of them ever included her in their activities, whether in or outside of school. In the beginning, Leticia had simply assumed that they had long-established groups that hung out together. But lately she was beginning to feel deeper issues might be involved. Even Dr. Bovard, the principal who had hired her, always smiled and nodded when they passed each other, but he rarely had a word to say to her; nor did the other faculty members.

Second, there were the students to contend with. Almost all of them were college bound—Leticia couldn't even imagine what would happen to one of them who decided *not* to go on to higher education. In this high-powered suburb, most teenagers were not only expected to graduate but to graduate with honors. People also assumed that many students would be offered some type of scholarship. Leticia had even overheard some parents talking about how they held their students back before sending them to kindergarten so they would be bigger, stronger, and smarter than kids at other schools in the area—giving them better chances at scoring those scarce academic or athletic scholarships!

That was exactly part of the problem that the Montgomery family was coming in to talk about today. Matthew's grade in her class had been slipping, and with the AP exam coming up next month, his parents were concerned about Matthew's overall academic standing. Yet, Leticia wondered if they had something else on their minds when they made the appointment.

"Hello, Ms. Granados," Mrs. Montgomery's now familiar voice rang out, interrupting Leticia's thoughts. Leticia offered up a silent prayer for help as she rose to greet the couple standing imposingly in her doorway.

"Oh, hello, Mr. and Mrs. Montgomery. Please come in and have a seat." Leticia smiled as naturally as she could, directing them to the chairs she had arranged. "Where is Matthew? Should we wait for him?"

"No," Mr. Montgomery said firmly, sitting stiffly in the chair next to his wife. Leticia admired the nice cut of his designer suit, noticing too that Mrs. Montgomery had on a particularly large gold necklace that gleamed brightly in the florescent lighting of the classroom.

Leticia returned to her seat. "Oh, I thought we'd agreed it would be good for Matthew to be here so we could all go over his work together."

"*We* decided it would be better to go over things with you alone," Mrs. Montgomery responded rather haughtily. "Besides, Matthew is well aware of the quality of his work—especially when he compares it to what he does for the many qualified teachers at this school."

"Well, then," Leticia added quickly, trying not to appear ruffled by Mrs. Montgomery's tone, thinking, Did she actually mean to insinuate that I'm not one of those qualified teachers?

"Listen," Mr. Montgomery interrupted. "Let's cut to the chase. I'm a busy investment banker, and I'm taking time out of my schedule to meet with you again on matters that really shouldn't even be an issue. Matthew has always been a straight A student, and now he has a B+ in your class. This is simply unacceptable, and we want you to change his grade right now. We've seen his work; it's excellent, as always. We believe that you are a bit inexperienced and have not set up an efficient grading system that reflects the high caliber of students here at Ridgecrest. Perhaps it is your own background or training—we don't want to judge that. You were educated at a high school in the Bronx, weren't you?"

Mr. and Mrs. Montgomery stared at Leticia, waiting for her to reply. Momentarily stunned, Leticia gaped back at them. Now they're definitely being insulting, she said to herself, trying to remain calm. Just because she hadn't been educated in a fancy suburban district didn't mean she was any less qualified to teach at Ridgecrest than the rest of the faculty. And they weren't simply *asking* her to change Matthew's grade; they were *telling* her what to do!

Oh, I knew Dr. Bovard should have been at this conference—but his secretary said he was too busy with meetings at the district office and that he knew I could handle this on my own, Leticia thought, her mind racing. She looked down at the stack of Matthew's papers, sorting through them to give herself a few more seconds before she responded. Please, God, don't let me say anything rash, she prayed silently.

"Here, look at this essay Matthew wrote on the environment. It was supposed to be a minimum of five pages in length, but he wrote a little over three." Leticia looked up hopefully at the parents, presenting the paper for them to see the B written across the top with her comments on how he could improve next time.

Barely glancing at her son's work, Mrs. Montgomery waved a ring-studded hand in front of the paper as if to dismiss it from her presence. "Really, Ms. Granados, do you penalize students for being concise with their thoughts? And, if you think about it, Matthew saved paper by only writing three pages—and that helps the environment, doesn't it?" Mrs. Montgomery smiled triumphantly at her husband for her own quick thinking.

Without responding, Leticia placed one of Matthew's recent exams in front of the parents, realizing she'd have to move quickly with this pair.

"Here is last week's exam. You'll notice that Matthew failed to answer the essay question about the African American scientist George Washington Carver, so he lost twenty points. I thought maybe he had simply run out of time, but when I questioned him about it later, he told me he didn't want to answer a racially based question."

"Yes," Mrs. Montgomery replied smugly, "we're proud of Matthew. He told us how you continually try to talk about minorities in class. Really, Ms. Granados, we don't have those racial problems here at Ridgecrest—but if you keep bringing these types of topics up, the young people might begin to have issues with those types of people."

Mr. Montgomery nodded approvingly at his wife, then he shifted his gaze to Leticia. "So, what's it going to be, young lady? Are you going to change Matthew's biology grade now, or do we have to take this matter elsewhere?"

"Elsewhere? What do you mean by that?"

"Just what I said. We've been in this district for years, and we give generously at the annual school auctions. We have no problem taking this matter up with Dr. Bovard, and I'm sure he will also encourage us to talk about some of your deficiencies with the superintendent. Or maybe you'd simply like to resolve this little grading situation now before things escalate. We're only thinking of Matthew. He's up for the valedictory circle, too, so we can't let your problems with assigning grades hurt his chances to get special honors at graduation!"

With that, Mr. Montgomery stood, motioning for his wife to do the same. Leticia stood up as well, though she felt her knees knocking under her skirt.

They're threatening and pressuring me, Leticia thought to herself, all because of a grade Matthew could bring up in the next few weeks if they actually put the pressure on him instead! I can't believe it! What can I do now? Leticia tried not to appear as shocked as she felt.

"I take your silence as a sign that you are refusing our suggestion. Well then, we'll just head down to the main office and see if Dr. Bovard is in." Mr. Montgomery marched toward the door, but Mrs. Montgomery held her ground, her dark eyes fixed on Leticia.

"By the way, Matthew mentioned that he spotted a Bible on your bookshelves. I think I might mention that to Dr. Bovard, too. Don't you know there is supposed to be separation of church and state? Really, you should have learned about that in your teacher-education program. But, based on what we've seen so far this year, you are obviously underprepared for many things!"

With that, Mrs. Montgomery turned on her stilettos and scurried out the door right behind her husband.

Leticia collapsed into her chair, physically and emotionally drained. She wondered how Dr. Bovard would respond to these influential parents and how, despite her tenure, this incident might affect her teaching record. Would Dr. Bovard add something negative to her teaching file? Would she be able to continue teaching the AP biology classes?

Perhaps even more surprising were some other thoughts that began to surface, thoughts that she had been suppressing for some time: Do I really want to continue teaching here at Ridgecrest—or do I even want to stay in the teaching profession at all?

Questions for Consideration

1. What do you think of Leticia's feelings about being excluded by the staff? Could she take any steps to try to fit in more? Are there some things that her coworkers should do to help her? If so, what are they?
2. Do you think that working in a school like Ridgecrest, with highly motivated students and well-to-do parents, is a good or bad situation? How might it be an advantage to teachers? What possible problems might they need to prepare for?
3. Did Leticia seem prepared for the meeting with Mr. and Mrs. Montgomery? Could she could have taken some additional measures to ensure a better outcome? Even if Dr. Bovard refused to attend the meeting, could she have enlisted someone else's help? If so, whose?
4. How did Leticia handle these parents' obviously rude comments? Would you act the same way if something similar happened to you? How does holding your tongue actually help you appear more professional?
5. How might Leticia's faith play a role in her decision-making processes? Why would changing a grade, even from a B+ to an A−, be a problem for her? What other ramifications could her changing the grade have?
6. Why did Mrs. Montgomery throw in the comment about a Bible being part of Leticia's collection of books in the classroom? Is it a problem for teachers to have religious books on the shelves in their classrooms? What types of books might it be problematic to have at school?
7. What kind of grading system do you plan to use as a teacher? Is it fair? How will it accurately represent student achievement in your class? What are some ways you can prepare in advance in order to avoid questions about your grading system?

For Further Exploration

Example: Have I ever experienced this type of pressure from someone at work? What kinds of issues did I have to deal with? Was I ultimately able to stand up for what I believed was the right decision? Would I handle matters in the same way again?

Explanation: How would I best explain my grading system to someone else? Can I back it up with proven methods or research? Is it important to consider the evaluation methods used by other teachers at my school, in my grade level, or in my department as I refine my own plan?

Exhortation: What can I do to encourage a good, healthy dialogue about grades with students and their parents? Are there ways to address this issue at the beginning of the school year to avoid potential problems later on?

Environment: How can I encourage all of my students to value achieving in my class? What kinds of recognitions and incentives will I have in addition to grades? Can I help my students—no matter what age—see the importance of doing well both now and in the future?

Experience: Can I include a lesson that teaches my students exactly what I do when grading their work? Perhaps we could all grade some papers together. Maybe I could give a math lesson that calculates several imaginary students' grades to see what happens when a test score is low or several homework assignments are missing. Or, could I have my students help design the next rubric for grading a project so they can see the specific expectations before they even start to work?

~

CHAPTER TEN

Religion, Politics, and Delicate Curricular Subjects

Companion none is like unto the mind alone; for many have been harmed by speech, through thinking, few or none.

—Sir Thomas Vaux, *Of a Contented Mind*, 1557

Initial Thoughts

In some teacher-preparation programs, it is common for students to prepare lesson plans during their coursework. Often these plans encompass several days, or even one to two weeks, and are written as units around a theme or event. In California, as in many other states, students also have to incorporate state standards and other kinds of curricular guidelines into the development of their units. Many students get to teach their planned unit either during their field experiences or, more often, during their extended student-teaching semester.

Deciding what to teach can be a serious endeavor with many facets. Some districts hand teachers strict curriculum programs and suggest that these educators, particularly the new ones, not deviate from them. Other districts are much more open to teacher initiative and experience. The curricula are more like guidelines than detailed blueprints, and teachers can incorporate innovative teaching units from outside sources to enliven the classroom in an attempt to interest and motivate the students, particularly older ones.

In an article in *California English* (1996), Infantino suggested that curriculum leadership and censorship are not very far apart. Noting that many veteran

English teachers prefer to retain the "tried and true" (or perhaps the *tired* and true), he stated that all teachers must be on guard so that that their practices remain relevant to the students they teach today, not yesterday. Curricula should be reviewed much more often than every ten years, or simply when the money for revising them becomes available.

Teacher educators over the years have been accused of lacking both knowledge and insight into curricular practices in K–12 schools. But other critics make the reverse accusation that these practitioners teach their students methods that are "too far out" or "not appropriate for our district." It sometimes seems that teachers in training get caught in the middle/muddle of juggling expectations—those of their professors on the one hand and those of the classrooms to which they are assigned on the other.

The case below is one such example. The student teacher wants to bring a well-planned unit into his eleventh-grade English curriculum. His university supervisor and methods teacher support such a plan and encourage him to try it. His cooperating teacher, however, denies the student teacher that opportunity, suggesting that the unit is inappropriate for the school circumstances. So, what is appropriate? Is it only the tried and true, or could there be some innovation that fits the curriculum but that a department or group of school administrators has not approved in advance?

Curriculum development and innovation certainly are not limited to issues of new versus experienced teachers. Departmental philosophies, central office priorities, school board viewpoints, and parental and community preferences all come into play when curricula are being revisited, no matter what the grade or geographic area. We have all read about the "reading wars" involving the most appropriate ways to instruct young students to read in English. The debate continues about how much evolutionary theory is appropriate to introduce in biology classes. And controversies over the inclusion or exclusion of particular books and stories in the study of literature are present every year in nearly every geographic area of the country (see National Committee against Censorship materials, for example).

At the heart of many of these discussions is often the appropriateness of certain materials or approaches for pupils' ages and grade levels. A second element involves the prevailing community attitudes as judged by the policies and politics of a particular district administration or school board. It is, after all, the right and duty of the board to make policy decisions and approve curricula, most often with the advice of the superintendent and his or her staff. However, pressures on boards of education do enter the picture, especially if a given board is elected by the community on a regular basis.

Teachers often feel conflicted about curricular decisions. They want to abide by the rules, yet they also know the pupils need to be motivated and exposed to materials that will stretch their thinking and their knowledge. In today's electronic age, newer and younger teachers often have skills and understandings that are closer to those of their students than are those of their more veteran colleagues and the community members who serve on school boards and committees. And so, the dilemmas continue. How can a student teacher move the curriculum forward without seeming so "out in space" that he or she will not be hired after student teaching or tenured after a probationary period?

The case of Mike Leblanc will test your ethical problem-solving skills on many levels. You and your teachers or mentors may have differing opinions about the case and will perhaps offer opposing suggestions. Curriculum development is an area in which you may or may not want to become involved. But if you decide not to become involved, you may become the victim rather than the protagonist of the story you write for yourself as a teacher.

Points to Ponder

Take time to reflect on the first chapter discussion of the "**3 S's**." The **Stakeholders** may become more invested when it comes to resolving delicate matters. Your past experiences with **Similar Scenarios** may impact your own current decision-making. Most importantly, how can you best use the **Self-Application** process so that your students also can learn how to handle delicate issues?

Case 8

The new year couldn't have started out any better for Mike Leblanc. He had just completed all of his preparatory work in education during his undergraduate program, with an English degree and twenty units of foundations and methods courses. After looking at his e-mail on January 2, he discovered that the School of Education had found a place for him to do his student teaching beginning January 15 and finishing in June. Rubideaux High School was located in a semirural area, about twenty-five miles from the mid-sized city where Mike had attended college.

Mike looked over the attachment Dr. Margaret Granger, his student-teaching supervisor, had sent him about the school. Rubideaux had twelve-hundred students in grades 9–12. The demographics revealed a mostly Caucasian student body, with about seventy-five students of African American descent, many of whose parents worked at the local mill. The town was located in what is often referred to as the Bible Belt, a descriptor that represents the mostly conservative religious views of the community members, which also impact the prevailing political beliefs of the people of this region.

As Mike read the details about his student-teaching assignment, he became more excited. He had always dreamed of becoming a teacher, and although he had enjoyed his time at the state college, he was ready to get started in his chosen profession. Mike knew there would undoubtedly be some challenges with this assignment, especially since he was not from this area originally and would now be working in an even smaller community than he was used to in his home up north. He had already noticed many differences in the region from the more diverse cultural, social, and religious traditions he had experienced while growing up in a large metropolitan area.

The assignments for Mike included two teaching periods of American literature with Lucas Peabody, a forty-eight-year-old, veteran teacher with a quarter century's worth of experience. He was a well-respected, local resident who returned to his own high school to teach English and monitor the debate team. Mr. Peabody had developed the eleventh-grade American literature curriculum ten years before, then had it approved by the department, the principal, and the local board of education. It was a classic college-preparatory curriculum featuring novels by Twain, Hemingway, Faulkner, Fitzgerald, and Steinbeck—and several other white male authors. Some short stories and poems by female writers were also included, and a few pieces written by people of color could be found in the fifteen-year-old literature anthology approved by the district.

Principal Lloyd Jenkins had been a teacher of special education at Rubideaux before being assigned as its principal just a few years before. His charges from the local school board were to raise test scores, especially in math, to get more students into college, and to run a tight, well-disciplined school. He had succeeded at the latter, but the school seemed still to be lagging in the first two areas.

Mike Leblanc had met Mr. Peabody and his second cooperating teacher, Gail Fletcher, in his observation experiences the previous semester. He liked both of the teachers and looked forward to learning from them, especially since each had a completely different teaching style. Gail Fletcher was thirty-two years old, taught ninth-grade English, and had been hired at Rubideaux six years before. She had completed her preparation at the State University Center about one hundred miles away and had taught for one year in a large district near the university. The mother of two young children, she and her husband decided she should take the offer at Rubideaux after her former school had to cut back its staff members, herself included. The couple thought that living in a smaller community like the one in which Rubideaux High School was located would be best for everyone, and Gail seemed to flourish in this environment.

Upon arrival at the school on January 15, both teachers gave Mike curriculum plans for the third quarter. He noted that Mr. Peabody's American literature program included the novel *The Great Gatsby*, while Mrs. Fletcher's ninth-grade curriculum included Hemingway's *The Old Man and the Sea*. Peabody's curriculum covered 1900 to 1940, taking a sequential historical approach, while Fletcher's seemed more eclectic, focusing on short stories from around the world and on novellas, accompanied by lots of writing instruction and production by the students. Mike felt comfortable in these settings, spending long hours each evening getting familiar with both teachers' curriculum units.

Two weeks into the semester, Mike approached Mr. Peabody about some new ideas he had for the curriculum.

"In my education program, I developed a unit that lasts about two weeks. It focuses on the Harlem Renaissance period of the 1920s and would be a great supplement to *Gatsby* and the other authors we study in February. Besides, February is Black History Month, and we could easily incorporate many famous African Americans into our study. What do you think?"

"I think not, Mike," Mr. Peabody responded rather abruptly. "What's the use in teaching that stuff anyway? We don't have many black students here at the school, and we certainly don't have many of those kids bound for college either. Plus, I don't have approval in the curriculum plan for this kind of material! We have to teach more classic literature because the colleges expect it, our principal expects it, and the parents expect it. Besides, the literature from that 1920s period isn't very good, as far as I know, and other than Langston Hughes, there aren't any authors worth our time. And even he isn't really that good."

Mike shifted back and forth on his feet uncomfortably, trying to decide what to say next. Before he could collect his thoughts, Mr. Peabody continued.

"I know you are new to the area, Mike, but you should have realized by now that this community is made up of a God-fearing, Bible-believing, politically conservative bunch of good folks. They would not take kindly to exposing their children to the radical stuff you'd be teaching. They also would not appreciate their kids studying literature that might rile up our black neighbors; we're all on good terms and really don't need any disruptions. And, Mike, I really don't think the principal or the school board would ever let us do this anyway. So now, if that's all, I need to get back to grading some quizzes."

Taken aback, Mike gathered himself for a response. He just knew that this material would be good for all of the students to experience, especially the African American kids who already seemed bored by the unit they had started. "Can we maybe think about it, Mr. Peabody? I'll show you the unit that I prepared and ask for your input and help in teaching it. You will find that it meets the curriculum expectations of the course and should really provide all students, not just the African American students, with an interesting mix of literature and the arts. What do you say?"

"I say forget it, Mike. Let's just get on with Gatsby for the next three weeks, maybe study a poem or two by Hughes, and then move into the Great Depression."

Great Depression seemed like a very appropriate term, since it described Mike's mood after this conversation. But Mike's depression soon shifted to anger. He couldn't believe Mr. Peabody's narrow-minded, racially insensitive views! Mike wasn't quite sure where to turn for help. He finally decided to call Dr. Granger, who not only was serving as his supervisor for student teaching but had also been one of his methods-class instructors.

Dr. Granger was a bit surprised when she picked up Mike's frantic voice-mail message. She had just completed teaching her last course of the day, a multicultural class for graduate students. Once she settled back in her office, she gave Mike a call.

"Mike, I'm so glad you picked up. You sounded pretty upset on the message you left. Why are you so surprised by Mr. Peabody's denial of your request? All of his training and teaching experience has been in this community, and he feels that he has an obligation to uphold its standards and structures. Teaching something like Harlem Renaissance literature goes well beyond his comfort zone. I'm sure he would tell you that the school board and the parents would strongly disapprove of bringing such violent, sex-filled, protest literature into Rubideaux's English curriculum."

"Well he strongly hinted at that, for sure," Mike added. "But you know, Dr. Granger, not all the literature from that time is offensive or revolutionary. Remember my unit plan from last semester? You said it was great and should be taught to students of all races. Why not here at Rubideaux?"

"Yes, I remember the unit, Mike. I also recall our discussion about being careful with your curricular choices. The appropriateness of timing, experience, and approval must be considered whenever something new is to be introduced into the curriculum. Mr. Peabody may not yet trust you enough to let you do the unit, especially since you have only been there for two weeks."

"That may be so, Dr. Granger, but I think it's the attitude more than the denial that has me upset! It seems to me that Mr. Peabody borders on holding racist beliefs and brings them into curricular decisions. Saying that there isn't much good literature from that period reveals a bias that teachers today shouldn't have, don't you agree?"

Dr. Granger was not about to step further into this fray over the phone. Side-stepping Mike's question, she asked, "What do you say about trying to set up a meeting on Monday with Mr. Peabody, you, and me? We might talk together about the positives and negatives of teaching all or part of your unit, and why it is or is not appropriate. We can also discuss in more general terms the notion of 'educating the whole person' by making students aware of the similarities among the hopes and ambitions of all people, which of course is one message to come out of that era. What do you say, Mike? Are you up to the challenge?"

"Sure, I am!" Mike replied, with a false bravado. "I'll tell Mr. Peabody that you want to meet together on Monday, and that you can be here at 3 p.m. Is that okay?"

"I'll be there, Mike," Dr. Granger answered. "Don't get your hopes up too high or get depressed thinking about these issues. All of us in teaching have faced censorship of one form or another in our careers, and this is a familiar one. We'll give it our best shot and see what happens. Call me to confirm when you've set up the meeting—or if you have anything else you want to discuss."

When Mike hung up from this call, his mind was still reeling, especially toward the worst-case scenarios: What if Peabody kicks me out of student teaching? Will my student teaching with Mrs. Fletcher be enough? What if the principal reports me to the university as a rabble-rouser and tells them I will never pass with my attitudes? And what if I accuse Mr. Peabody of censorship or racism—that won't get me anywhere! He's never going to change his views at his age. Maybe I'd better call Dr. Granger back and tell her to forget the meeting. I'll just teach his old curriculum, get my A, and be satisfied. . . . Nah, that will never do! Of course, I could go and talk to Peabody right now, before I lose my nerve.

Mike stacked up the papers he had been working on and put them in his briefcase, along with his Harlem Renaissance unit. Then, off he went, straight to Mr. Peabody's office to see if he was still there. "I just have to get this off my chest—it's what's best for the students!" he repeated to himself, all the way into the lion's den.

Questions for Consideration

1. How might the conversation go between Mike, Lucas Peabody, and Dr. Margaret Granger? What ethical arguments could convince Mr. Peabody to allow all or part of the Harlem Renaissance unit to be taught?
2. How do the religious and political beliefs of the community, and perhaps of Mr. Peabody, affect the literature curriculum in this case? Can you think of examples that you have studied or experienced yourself when religious or political beliefs influenced what was being taught in the K–12 curriculum?
3. When (if ever) might censorship of curriculum offerings be appropriate? What is the difference between teaching age-appropriate materials and censoring curricular offerings? Who should decide these critical issues?
4. Describe some ways in which a student teacher or beginning teacher might be able to introduce new material into a school's curriculum.
5. What is a university supervisor's role in convincing a cooperating teacher to allow a student teacher some freedom in curricular matters? What is the role of mentor teachers in the curriculum planning of beginning teachers?
6. Have you seen an inspiring movie about a teacher who makes the curriculum come alive? Try viewing *Dead Poets Society* or reading or viewing *Freedom Writers*, then reflect on this chapter again.

For Further Exploration

Example: What does it say to pupils when materials written by people from many cultural backgrounds are included in curricula at all levels?

Explanation: As a student teacher, should I take the risk of explaining to my pupils the cooperating teacher's decisions about curricular or teaching issues when I disagree with them? Why or why not?

Exhortation: Group projects and independent research are ways to allow more student-centered activities. What group projects or outside research activities have I tried or will I try this year?

Environment: What will prevent me from becoming a two-by-four teacher—one who teaches only material found between the two covers of a book and within the four walls of the classroom?

Experience: Would I accept an opportunity to serve on a curriculum revision committee as a beginning teacher? What might be some advantages and disadvantages of doing so?

~

CHAPTER ELEVEN

Relationship Red Flags

Four be the things I am wiser to know: Idleness, sorrow, a friend, and a foe.

—Dorothy Parker, *Enough Rope*, 1927

Initial Thoughts

In our note to you at the beginning of the book, you may recall that we mentioned the importance of relationships to the everyday educator. It goes without saying that teaching is an interpersonal profession; if it were not for other people, we would not have jobs. Schools cannot exist without staff members to run them, parents to support them (financially as well as personally), and students to fill them. Although these varied relationships are some of the brightest aspects of the profession, they can occasionally become problematic.

Since so many of us enter the field of education because we like people, have high hopes for our students, and want to dedicate ourselves to improving the lives of others, it seems essential that we should have some basic guidelines on how to achieve successful relationships with those around us. Unfortunately, we often do not get much guidance. Most colleges and universities have so much to teach in so little time (our theme in case 3), and many schools of education simply hope that those entering the teaching profession already have appropriate interpersonal skills. Thankfully, this is generally true, although many of us might actually appreciate learning some extra skills to add to our "relationship tool kits."

In this and the three subsequent cases, we aim to help you develop relationship skills as we delve very specifically into critical interpersonal issues that you might encounter. For now, we are going to suggest to you the three most essential tools to get you started building and maintaining positive, healthy interpersonal connections with people. These three skills are

1. developing good boundaries
2. improving discernment about others
3. increasing awareness of "red flag warnings" about potentially unhealthy or unsafe relationships

In addressing the *first vital skill*, developing boundaries, clinical psychologists Cloud and Townsend (1992) suggest that people who want to have great personal and professional relationships must first learn how to establish appropriate, healthy boundaries. "Boundaries are anything that helps to differentiate you from someone else, or shows where you begin and end" (Cloud and Townsend 1992, 33). The clinicians also explain that establishing boundaries is essential for successful living because they help us keep "the good in and the bad out" (Cloud and Townsend 1992, 33).

Before someone builds a house, school, or office building, the boundary lines must be established, requiring much prior thought and effort. The same is true in all of our relationships. If we take the time to decide thoughtfully (1) who we are and what we want our personal boundaries to be, and (2) how we will deal with others who come into contact with us and our boundaries, then we have taken the initial steps toward establishing balanced relationships.

In other words, we can choose to go through life "willy-nilly"—bouncing from day to day, just letting things happen. But the chances are slim that this type of free-floating, disorganized philosophy will have definite, organized results. However, if we decide to spend some time thinking more about who we are and what we want out of life, this *intentional approach* will more than likely lead to some *intentional end results*.

As an educator you can choose to think through the types of relationships that you will have as you begin your career and about how you want to see those interpersonal experiences play out over the course of time.

- How do you want to interact with your students?
- What kind of relationships do you hope to establish with fellow teachers, staff members, and administrators?
- Will you have a plan in place to engage your students' parents and caregivers?

This is also the best time for you to consider your own interpersonal integrity, particularly as it involves professional relationships. At no other time in history have we seen so many educators cross boundary lines of appropriate behavior—especially involving students—than in this past decade. Indeed, some school districts are so concerned with the rapid rise in misconduct that they are implementing programs in ethics training for their staff members (see www.ethicsinstitute.com, for instance).

You need to be aware that although you may have already established excellent boundary lines concerning how you will relate with students, some of the young people in your care will not have learned these same valuable lessons at home. For example, you will have children in your classes who have been abused, physically and emotionally. They will have very fuzzy boundaries, if any, and will tend to seek attention from others, including teachers, sometimes in inappropriate ways.

At this juncture, we would like to say a few words to those of you working in high school settings. Many teachers begin their careers when they are young and close in age to the high school pupils, which sometimes creates difficulties in establishing boundaries with these students, who may only be five or six years younger. Some beginning teachers struggle with being *friendly* with their students without being *their friend*. This critical fine line must be established early so that you, as a student teacher or a new teacher, can not only earn student respect but also prevent any chance for misconduct—or rumored misconduct. Remember, although your chronological ages may be close for a short while, these young people are in your professional charge—and you are expected to respond professionally in all interactions with them.

In addition, we would like you to consider how you will react when you have encounters with "not-so-pleasant people." As much as we might not want to think about potential negative experiences with others, there are individuals in the world who are difficult to be around, even in generally pleasant places like elementary, middle, and high school campuses. You will have students who are challenging—academically, emotionally, and socially. You will more than likely come across colleagues who are cranky, cantankerous, or even downright confrontational. And what will you do when some parents, like the ones you read about in case 7, try to push your buttons and boss you around or become outraged by how you have graded their children?

The *second vital skill* that you can begin to work on now is discernment. In the course of your career, you will encounter some individuals who are not only problematic but also unhealthy to be around. Cloud and Townsend (1995) have authored a book about "safe people" and explain how we can develop better relationships by learning how to identify individuals who have good character qualities and avoid those who don't. For instance, people who possess many of the values and morals that we discuss in this book are readily identified by their attitudes and actions. Honesty, integrity, respect for others, tolerance, courtesy, and responsibility are characteristics you can notice as you interact with these emotionally and relationally healthy individuals.

Learning the art of discernment takes lots of time spent interacting with others. It is also invaluable to find two or three mentors whom you trust to help you with processing relationship issues—both good and bad. Often these mentors are older, more experienced individuals who have spent a great amount of time honing their own relationship skills. These mentors could include members of your family, such as a parent, grandparent, or another relative that you trust. You might have developed a professional relationship with a professor with whom you feel comfortable discussing ideas or problematic situations in your life. Many newer teachers still call or e-mail the cooperating teachers from their student-teaching days to get input about day-to-day teaching issues or solving problems they encounter at their own school sites. No matter how you look at it, surrounding yourself with a few sage individuals will be a big plus as you journey down the sometimes rocky road of relationships.

Finally, the *third vital skill* to add to your relationship repertoire is the ability to develop an awareness of "red flag warnings." By this we mean learning to hear that small voice inside that sometimes says, "Hey, wait a minute—something isn't right here!" When you hear that voice or feel uncomfortable in a situation, you need to listen carefully to this internal warning system. Some people are more tuned in than others, so listening to yourself may be a new skill set that you need to exercise more than you have in the past.

Red flags are especially important when it comes to certain rare, yet extremely challenging, interpersonal contacts we may make over the years. M. Scott Peck, in his pivotal book *People of the Lie: The Hope for Healing Human Evil* (1998), discusses the psychological issues that explain why some people are not only unsafe but also potentially dangerous. While most of us will never have long-term exposure to individuals like those Peck describes, his book has often been recommended to anyone who spends a majority of his or her career interacting with people.

As we have stated before, most of your teaching experiences, including relationships with others, should be extremely positive. But you must be prepared for almost anything when it comes to working with human beings! Dorothy Parker, the American author and poet, understood this all too well. From a rocky childhood, including losing her mother before she was five and her father at thirteen, through three tumultuous marriages, Ms. Parker experienced the best and worst of human relationships. Her Jewish background,

Protestant stepmother, and Catholic grade school education also formed some of the unusual boundary lines that she established for her professional as well as her personal life—some were good boundaries; others were not as good.

Her poignant quote above should serve as a reminder as you read this next case study that it is indeed important to know things beforehand—as well as to have a plan of action when circumstances don't go exactly as you had hoped! You will soon discover that it will be extremely beneficial for your career to make good decisions when it comes to your own private actions as well as your interpersonal interactions.

In our years within educational settings—from private to parochial to public schools—we have certainly observed and been involved in the gamut of interpersonal relationships. We've had amazingly gifted students who enjoyed our teaching and absorbed as much as they could in our courses. We have also had kids in our classes who worked hard to dance around assignments, fake parent signatures, and lie to us outright without blinking an eye. Many caregivers have been outstanding, the types who should write books on the art of parenting so the rest of us can benefit from their examples. Then there were others who, like a splinter in a thumb, went out of their way to rub us the wrong way . . . sometimes on a regular basis!

Of course, there were our colleagues, by and large the greatest treasures to our growing professional skills as they shared bountifully from their experiences and their own educational materials to help us build up our own. Still, beside these treasured gems, there were also some "diamonds in the rough." *Very* rough! A few simply chose to be bad tempered and mean-spirited; a handful also seemed to enjoy spreading rumors, backbiting, and even taking things from other teachers just to spite them! "Unprofessional" is the kindest word we can use right now to describe these "unsafe" individuals.

How about you, our readers? What have you experienced when it comes to relationships thus far? Have you had good, trustworthy interactions with others in your life? Perhaps, like Ms. Parker, you've had your own share of rough spots—including dealing with unsafe or unhealthy people. Have you been able to move on from these situations and establish sound boundaries for yourself? Do you feel like you need more help with discerning good character traits in others or becoming more sensitive to red flags in relationships? There's no better time than the present to improve these skill sets.

You may want to add a list of your own strengths and weakness to your notebook or journal right now. Carefully consider those areas that you would like to improve on in the days ahead. We also recommend that you choose one of the aforementioned books to get this process started or select another resource from those recommended in appendixes B and C.

Now, with all of these ideas swirling in your mind, let's take a look at how well Heather McBride uses the three skills we've just discussed in her relationships at Francis Xavier Academy.

Points to Ponder

Stakeholders: Who is going to be most impacted when there are problems with relationships in educational settings? ***Self-Application:*** How do my healthy boundaries help everyone around me?

Case 9

The buzz of the playground noise hummed in Heather McBride's ears as she watched a group of kids move through the hopscotch pattern on the blacktop. She smiled as she thought back to her own elementary school days, longing for recess so she could play with her friends. Indeed, Francis Xavier Academy reminded her of the parochial school she had attended just across town: beautiful grounds and well-kept brick buildings, with the chime of chapel bells calling everyone to daily mass.

She hadn't planned on teaching in a private school, let alone in the same diocese where she had attended school for so many years herself. But then her mom passed away from cancer during Heather's sophomore year of college, so she moved home to help her dad care for two of her siblings, who were still in high school. She was actually happy to return home; the loss of her mom hit her harder than she had imagined, so the familiarity of family life, the city where she'd grown up, and being among friends comforted her. She had finished her degree and teaching credential before she knew it, and then Francis Xavier Academy had contacted her about her interest in teaching third grade.

During her springtime interview at the academy, Heather instantly liked Sister Katherine, the principal of this highly respected P–8 parochial school. A few weeks later, at the end of July, she signed her first teaching contract and was assigned a room on the first story of the building where the primary students were housed. She spent weeks organizing materials left behind by the previous third-grade teacher, who reportedly had left for a higher paying job at a nearby public school.

Now that October was nearly over, Heather was finally beginning to feel like she had a handle on the busy daily schedule and the curricula she needed to be covering with her energetic bunch of students. She spent a lot of late nights preparing, and many weekends too. No time for a social life right now, Heather thought to herself.

Yet, her eyes wandered across the playground toward Cody Smithson. He, too, had been hired this year to teach fifth grade, leaving a public school position for some unknown reason. There had been rumors within the faculty about the "extenuating circumstances" that may have caused his dismissal, but no one knew for sure.

"He is awfully cute, isn't he?" a cheerful voice rang out. Heather quickly turned to find Maureen Zander, a fourth-grade teacher who had been at the academy almost thirty years, standing beside her with a big grin on her face.

"Oh, hi, Maureen. You can sure sneak up on a person."

"Years of practice, my dear. I've learned that you've got to be quick and quiet on your feet to keep these kiddos on their toes, too. You wouldn't believe how many notes I've intercepted without making a sound to forewarn the poor child I snuck up on. Anyways, I couldn't help but notice your gaze wandering toward Mr. Smithson over there. He is a hottie—isn't that what your generation calls them?"

Heather laughed. "That's the term—at least right now. And, yes, he is cute. I just wish I knew more about him—like why he left his last job, for instance."

"Well, I'm not one to gossip, but I think he may have run into trouble because he's been far too touchy with his students. Sister Katherine has already spoken to him about hugging his students, especially the girls. There's a new policy in the diocese about that now, you know. Personally, I don't like the rule. . . . I mean, if a child needs a hug or a pat on the back, aren't we supposed to be there for them? I guess I'm old-fashioned in that regard. But male teachers need to be especially careful these days."

"Well, there are some female teachers in the news lately who should have taken that advice too."

"You're right—like Lexi Simpson, whom Cody replaced. Why she posted those pictures on the Internet of herself partying in the Caribbean, I'll never know!" Disdain was evident in Maureen's voice. And who could blame her? Lexi's exploits had even made it onto some of the cable news shows! Heather had been aghast when she discovered that a teacher in this well-respected diocese had made such a foolish decision, one that not only hurt her own career but also made everyone in the community look bad.

"I don't think Lexi will be able to get a job in this area again after that fiasco!" Maureen added.

"By the way, Maureen, how did you know that Cody had to speak to Sister Katherine?" Heather inquired.

"Oh, I've got my sources. You'll see. Once you've been at a school for some time, you'll find out who can give you good information . . . and who you need to be careful of. Uh oh! Speak of the devil, here comes one right now." Maureen clammed up but inclined her head toward the nearby chapel.

Heather turned in that direction to see Lynne Gregory, the art teacher, heading toward them. Heather looked back at Maureen who simply winked.

"Hi, girls, what are you up to?" Lynne's melodic voice sang out as she neared the twosome. "Isn't it a great fall day? The trees are aflame with color, the breeze is brisk, and the scenery is simply *gorgeous!*"

That's when Heather noticed Lynne's gaze also drifting toward Cody. Then Lynne flounced her long, auburn hair over her shoulder and flashed a huge smile in Cody's direction. Cody, who had been playing basketball with some of his fifth graders, immediately noticed Lynne's attention and waved, looking a bit surprised to find three women staring at him. He went back to shooting hoops after one of his students called out, "Hey, Mr. Smithson, let's go. Recess is almost over."

"Yes, too bad recess is almost over." Lynne sighed rather loudly. "I could have stood here and enjoyed this view for a long time. Oh well, I should scoot. I'll see you later, Heather. I've got a lovely art project to start with your third graders this afternoon. Bye, Maureen."

And with that, Lynne drifted off toward the main buildings, but not before she shot another gleaming smile in Cody's direction.

"You've got to watch out for that gal," Maureen whispered to Heather, nodding knowingly.

"Who, Lynne? What do you mean? "

"She's the school 'cougar'—you know, the older woman who preys on the younger male teachers. Cody is her *new* target, so if you do like him, be careful. After all, she's the *real* reason that there was an opening in third grade for you."

"What?" Heather was shocked. "I thought Tonya left because she got a better-paying public school job."

"Well, that certainly must have taken the sting out of the situation, I'm sure," Maureen remarked. "But Lynne made things pretty miserable for Tonya after she simply commented to Lynne that she liked the music teacher, Mr. Jefferson. Lynne was livid because she'd been flirting with Jerry Jefferson for two years without any luck. Unfortunately, his job got cut, and he left. It's sad, because the music program was stellar under his direction, but you know how finances go in parochial schools these days."

Heather interrupted Maureen before she drifted off onto another topic. "But Lynne seems so nice. She's been extremely helpful since I've been here, even giving me a stack of posters so I could decorate my room nicely. Are you sure Tonya's departure was her fault?"

"Oh, you know I don't like to spread rumors, but *everyone* knows Lynne's reputation. And as much as Sister Katherine, bless her, has tried to tone Lynne's activities down, I'm afraid that gal isn't going to change her ways any time soon. You'd think she'd settle down after what we all went through with Lexi's mess-up. Just be careful, Heather. I'd like you to stay here a while."

With that final warning, Maureen headed toward the large number four on the blacktop where her students had already started to line up. Heather had been so lost in thought that she hadn't even heard the bell that signaled the end of recess. She finally heard her third graders calling out her name, so she walked over to where they had gathered on the blacktop to lead them back to the classroom.

The afternoon went by swiftly, the last hour of which included Lynne's art lesson. She had brought in a beautiful basket of fall leaves, explaining the different types to Heather's students in her melodic way, and then got them busy tracing the leaves onto colorful construction paper. Yet, Heather found herself being surprisingly cautious around Lynne, especially after Maureen's warning.

Once the students had cleaned up after their art project, Heather reminded them about the homework packets they needed to take home over the weekend. She then escorted the kids out the door, returned to her desk, and plopped down in the cozy rolling chair. Heather's thoughts returned to Cody Smithson again. He seemed nice enough, but could he really have been let go from his previous school because of a "touching problem" with one of his students? What would she do if he did ask her out on a date? Would Lynne start to cause problems for her? And could she really trust that Maureen was telling the truth about all of the things she'd shared?

Heather's thoughts were interrupted when she heard a sharp rapping at the doorway.

"Uh, Ms. McBride, do you have a minute?"

Heather looked up to see Dr. Chad Aimsly, a parent of one of her third graders, standing inside the classroom.

"Of course, Dr. Aimsly, come on in." Heather stood and moved toward the door.

"Oh, please, call me Chad." He hesitated, taking another step inside. "I have a question for you—actually, it might seem a little awkward, but I've been eager to ask you something—well, uh."

Heather figured it must have something to do with the progress reports that had gone out that week. "Sure, Dr.—I mean—Chad. You can ask me anything," she said reassuringly, smiling as she walked forward.

Then, out of the blue, Dr. Aimsly posed this question: "Well, I wondered if you'd like to go out with me this weekend. I really like you a lot, and I know you are single too. What about dinner and a movie on Saturday?"

Heather stopped in her tracks, the smile that had been on her face slowly dissipating. She had no clue that this would be Dr. Aimsly's question since they had hardly spoken to each other in the two months that Heather had been at the school. As she quickly struggled to come up with a good reply, she thought to herself, A date? Kiley's dad is asking me out on a date! As if I don't have enough things on my mind!

Questions for Consideration

1. What do you think of Maureen Zander? Is she really "not one to gossip?" Is she, as Dorothy Parker says, a friend or foe . . . or someone in between? How could her insights help or hurt Heather?

2. How might Heather's personal life, especially the loss of her mother, impact her relationships with others?

3. What kind of boundaries would you recommend that Heather think about establishing before she goes any further in her relationships at school?

4. Who might be good mentors for Heather to include in processing some of the relationship issues that have already occurred at Francis Xavier Academy? How can she avoid gossiping and spreading rumors while still trying to get help on how to handle her own interactions with others on staff?

5. Which stakeholders have already been impacted by Lexi's posting pictures on the Internet? How have the departures of Tonya and Jerry Jefferson potentially impacted the school? What type of problems can occur in a school that has such turnover in staff from year to year?

6. How is the labeling of people in this story problematic? Could the use of labels by someone be a "red flag" to you? What other red flag warnings does this scenario include?

7. Are these types of relationship problems more prevalent at smaller or larger schools, or does the size of the school really matter? How might

relationships vary depending upon the size of the staff that you will be working with?

8. What should Heather do about the date request by the parent of one of her students? Why?

For Further Exploration

Example: When was the last time I struggled with a relationship issue? Did it have anything to do with the boundaries—or the lack of them—that I had in my life? Was I able to discern clearly the character traits that could have forewarned me about potential problems? How did I do in recognizing the "red flag warnings" at that time?

Explanation: What are my personal boundaries? Do I feel comfortable with them, and can I stand by them when I need to set limits with others? How would I explain these as well as my professional boundaries to others?

Exhortation: As a teacher or leader, I want to be able to encourage my students and colleagues to establish healthy, safe boundaries for themselves. How can I urge them to do so, other than by personal example? Are there specific conversations that might be good introductions to this type of discussion?

Environment: My classroom should be the first place where students can observe appropriate boundaries—with me as well as with their fellow classmates. What kind of system can I have in place that will allow them to experience good boundaries on a daily basis? How can I help them become aware of positive character traits that they can be developing?

Experience: Since identifying red flags isn't easy even for adults, how can I help my students understand what red flags look and feel like? Can I provide them with appropriate short stories, skits, or video clips that will start good conversations about how to identify potential problems in relationships—and then work to develop skill sets for making decisions in problematic situations?

CHAPTER TWELVE

~

The Dating Game

The union of the mathematician with the poet, fervor with measure, passion with correctness, this surely is the ideal.

—William James, *Clifford's Lectures and Essays*, 1879

Initial Thoughts

In December 1965, what might be considered a prototype for present-day reality television hit the airwaves for the first time. *The Dating Game*, hosted by Jim Lange, had a simple premise: a single guy had thirty minutes to ask three gals hidden behind a partition a series of questions. Then, the contestant chose one woman to take out on a "dream date." Sometimes the roles were reversed, with a female contestant asking three men questions in the hopes of finding "Mr. Right." The show became so popular, especially among singles, that ABC ran it until 1974. An updated version of *The Dating Game* later returned to the airwaves, minus the 1960s flower-power set, and it was also received warmly by the viewing public.

The show was clever and cute, with often comical questions. It naturally attracted the television audience because all of us have had the uncomfortable experience of trying to make small talk or figuring out how to get a date with someone else. Perhaps one of the best parts of *The Dating Game* show came when the participant selected his or her "bachelor" or "bachelorette" from behind the curtain, and viewers could see their reactions when their eyes met for the first time.

Yes, the laws of attraction run deep and strong—and not just among television watchers. Humans are naturally wired for relationships, and often we don't know when, as the saying goes, "lightning might strike." Although such an occurrence may sound appealing, particularly if you've been single for some time and are ready to find a significant other, we are going to ask you to pause for a moment, as they did back in the days of early television programming, and take a station break. We have several important messages to convey before you ever even think about dating a colleague on your school site.

Now, we don't mean to suggest that great relationships haven't been formed among coworkers, or that some of these relationships can't develop into long-lasting ones. Indeed, both of your authors know many people who, over the years, have fallen in love while teaching together at various elementary, middle, and high school campuses. But, once again, we would be remiss if we didn't forewarn you that these friends and colleagues of ours also had to cross some delicate ground carefully as they began their own "dating game."

First and foremost, professional conduct must be considered before you simply jump into any interpersonal relationship. You need to ask yourself a key question from the get-go: how will this relationship impact my students?

Hopefully you're saying to yourself, "Dr. Infantino and Dr. Wilke, of course I'm going to think about my students first!" (You can add the "Duh!" if you'd like; it won't hurt our feelings.)

Our reply to that is a resounding "Yeah!" That's what we hoped for! But, believe it or not, that type of thought pattern is not always typical. If it were, we wouldn't have received a phone call a few years ago from an angry cooperating teacher (a single mother of two) who had just broken up with her much-younger student teacher and now wanted him removed from her classroom. Their working relationship had become so strained that she wouldn't talk to him, and the high schoolers in their care were becoming upset as a result.

Yet, life happens, and fortunately for these two educators, they were able to stick the rest of the semester out successfully for the good of their students.

We would like to help you avoid this type of painful scenario now, well before you ever go out on a first date with anyone at your school site. Thinking through the policy you will have about dating coworkers—or anyone else for that matter—is an essential process as you begin your new profession. And what if a single parent decides to ask you out on a date, as in the scenario that Heather McBride encountered in case 9? Have you thought about what you would do if this situation ever arose?

Some employers actually have policies in place that help employees establish appropriate boundaries, but many employers do not. Even if such policies exist, you must inevitably decide how you are going to handle all relationship issues.

With your students in mind, you must also think about your professional ethics. How might dating someone at your school impact your day-to-day teaching? Will you be more distracted than you would like? Can you separate your personal and professional feelings, especially if problems occur in the relationship? Remember, you've worked extremely hard to get where you are today, and you don't want anything—or anyone—to put that status at risk.

Finally, exceptional educators always consider the stakeholders involved. What will other colleagues think about a relationship? Will dating this individual cause a problem with someone else at your school or in your department? What about in the administration or at the district office? Might someone on staff be concerned about your association with this person? How about the parents of students? Will you be able to conduct yourself in such a way that they will have no reason to question your care and concern for their children?

Yes, we may seem to be bombarding you with as many questions as you might get on a quiz show. But we'd much rather that you think about these types of realities now, before they turn into a dramatic dilemma down the road. After all, as William James warns us in the verse above, opposites do attract. And people are rarely prepared for when and where lightning does indeed strike!

In fact, think about your own dating history for a few moments. How did things start up for you in your last relationship? Were you ready for it, or did things kind of sneak up on you? What about an interpersonal relationship that didn't go so well? Was it difficult to end? How did you handle things after the breakup? How difficult would it have been if you had also had to face this person at work every day, all day? Or maybe you did break up with a coworker! What kind of problems did you face? Were you still able to maintain a professional relationship with that person?

While these thoughts are fresh in your mind, we invite you to spend some time reviewing the case study below. As you will discover, the two friends in this scenario had both taken a course on ethics, but one of them obviously forgot some of the major tenets she had studied. As you read about their decision-making processes (or lack thereof), consider the priorities you want to establish for your own dating life so that your professional position will never be in jeopardy!

Points to Ponder

Stakeholders: Have you ever dated a colleague? Did other co-workers at previous job sites have successful dating relationships? How did things work out? *Stakeholders:* Were other people understanding of the romantic relationship? How might they have been affected?

Case 10

"Oh, Jenna, I'm so glad I caught you! I've got to talk to someone right now!"

Jenna Jelenick clung to her cell phone as she quickly tossed her backpack on the passenger seat of her VW and closed the door. "What's happened, Lindsay? Is everything okay?"

Even as Jenna asked the question, she knew something was wrong with her friend. After rooming together for two years in college, Jenna recognized the strain in Lindsay Richardson's voice. Although they lived several hundred miles apart now, they kept in regular contact despite their busy teaching schedules.

"No, everything is not okay. I think I'm going to get fired!" Lindsay's frantic voice choked on the last few words, and she began sobbing on the other end of the line.

"Hold on, Lindsay. Let me get into my car so we can talk privately." Jenna maneuvered to the driver's side door and hopped in. "Okay, now calm down for a minute—take some deep breaths. Tell me what on earth is going on."

"Oh, Jenna, I really, really blew it! You know that cute boyfriend I was telling you about? Well, I didn't tell you everything. First of all, he's the assistant principal at the school here . . . and, oh my gosh, I hate to even say it, but he's . . . he's also married!"

"What!" Jenna blurted out, then regretted her response. There was no need to upset Lindsay any more than she already was—but married? Her friend was dating a married administrator?

"Okay, okay," Jenna tried to remain calm herself. "Hold on now—so you made a mistake and dated a married guy. Why should that get you fired? Are you sure you're not overreacting? People date each other at work all the time, and nothing happens to them."

"Well, that may be true in some jobs, but here it isn't that easy. The town is small, and everyone seems to know everyone else's business. Plus, I kind of made a scene in front of the school office yesterday when I found out Tom wasn't divorced like he said he was. I told him off right then and there, and some kids overheard. I guess they told their parents, and those parents called Mrs. Jackson, our principal, first thing this morning. She sent a substitute to take over for me as soon as the bell rang, and I spent an hour with her, having to explain everything. Jen, it's so embarrassing."

Jenna could hear Lindsay sobbing again on the other end of the phone. Oh my gosh, she thought to herself. What can I say? What a mess. And of all people, Lindsay should have known better. We took that ethics course with Dr. Nguyen . . . and he warned us about the dangers of these kinds of relationships. Jenna tried to think quickly about what to say next.

"Lindsay, it's okay. I'm here for you. Try to calm down a bit. Maybe things aren't as bad as you think. You know how at first situations can seem horrible, and then they're better by the next day. You know, like that song that says, 'Hold on for one more day, things will go your way.'"

After a few more sobs on the other end of the line, Lindsay finally spoke. "Well, maybe you're right. Mrs. Jackson was pretty upset today—she even had Tom take the rest of the day off. She said the district might put him on administrative leave. Maybe he will be the one to get in trouble, the dirty rat! Married! Can you believe he lied to me like that?"

For the next fifteen minutes, Lindsay revealed to Jenna the rest of the details about the relationship that she had been withholding for the past few months. Evidently, Tom had first pursued her, although Lindsay said she'd been reluctant to start any relationship with a coworker since she was so new at Menlo Elementary School. After work one Friday in October, she finally agreed to meet Tom at a local Mexican restaurant for happy hour. They ended up talking for hours, discovering that despite their age difference of twelve years, they seemed to have a lot in common. Lindsay felt flattered that a handsome man like Tom was interested in her, and he seemed so honest and open—unlike most of the guys she tended to meet.

Jenna asked if Tom had told Lindsay directly that he was divorced, and Lindsay said that he had. But now after thinking things over, Lindsay realized he'd also requested that she keep their romance a secret at school. He had explained that the divorce was pretty recent, so he didn't want anyone on his staff to start rumors about her moving in on him so quickly.

"Yeah, well, I guess I know now why he wanted to keep things such a secret. He's still got a wife and three kids at home."

"Wow, what a jerk!" Jenna sympathized with her friend's plight, but she still was worried about the precarious situation. Since neither woman was tenured in her respective district, they had been forewarned to be extremely careful about their conduct.

"I wish I could come and see you so we could talk in person." Jenna added.

"I know—me too. How are things going back home?" Lindsay asked.

"Good," Jenna replied carefully, not wanting to sound too happy given Lindsay's current circumstances. "I really like my first graders, and the rest of the staff seems pretty close. I hope I'm fitting in with them. Many of the faculty have been here since the school opened ten years ago."

"Oh, you'll be fine. I think you've described part of my problem, though," Lindsay added.

"What do you mean?"

"Well, the teachers here have been working together for years too, and I've already seen a few of them give me some strange looks as they passed me in the hallway right before I called you. I think they already know about Tom and me."

"You mean you're still at school?" Jenna asked.

"Yeah, Mrs. Jackson had me stay in the office today, but she wants me back in the classroom tomorrow. 'Until further notice' were her last words to me."

"Hum, well, I think it's a good sign that she wants you back in your classroom." Jenna tried to sound as positive as possible.

"I guess you're right. Hey, I should let you go. Can I call you later?"

"Of course! Give me a buzz in an hour or so. I'll be home by then, so we can talk more, okay?"

Jenna's wishful thinking, however, couldn't undo the snowball that had already begun forming in the Menlo Elementary School community. Evidently, Tom and Lindsay's relationship had not been so secret after all. In fact, rumors of Tom's infidelity had been rampant for years. He seemed to be a serial dater of the younger female faculty members in this small community. Mrs. Jackson had been newly assigned to the school, in part, to handle the assistant principal better than her predecessor had. Tom already had been placed on administrative leave once before when he was discovered kissing a female teacher in the parking lot instead of supervising a sixth-grade dance. The district office had allowed him to resume his position after placing a letter of warning in his employment file. The untenured female teacher had been let go immediately.

Concerned parents continued to bombard both Mrs. Jackson and the superintendent's offices with calls. A few angry parents even stormed into the district office to complain in person. Perhaps most damaging were the reports given by the students who had witnessed Lindsay's heated confrontation in front of the school office. Several of them repeated, verbatim, the words that had been exchanged—including a few expletives that Lindsay had used in the argument.

Finally, a few days later, Jenna's cell phone rang again.

"Hi, Lindsay, how are you? I've been so worried." Jenna exclaimed.

"Hi, Jen, I'm alright—I guess I should have called you yesterday, but it's taken some time for all of this to sink in."

"All of what? What's happened?" Jenna was worried.

"Well, the good news is that I still have a job—for now. But I've got to go to an important meeting at the district office on Monday. Some people are making a stink about my relationship with Tom. Mrs. Jackson informed me today that I will get to tell my side of the story to the superintendent and a few other district officials. I found out that Tom has been placed on administrative leave for two weeks, and he will get to take a new position at the district office in the curriculum department after that. I can't believe he's still going to have a job after what he's done to me."

Jenna felt very sorry for her friend, but she also thought about how Tom's wife and kids might be feeling right now too.

"So, Lindsay, did Mrs. Jackson give you any idea about what might happen?"

"Yes. She told me they may dismiss me right then and there, or I might be allowed to finish out the school year. She also told me not to get my hopes up about teaching for the district next year."

"Oh, Lindsay, I'm so sorry."

"Yeah, I wish I'd paid more attention to what Dr. Nguyen told us about dating people at school!"

Me too, Jenna agreed silently. After they ended their phone conversation, Jenna sat on the couch in her apartment wondering what the consequences of Lindsay's decisions might be. Could a simple dating scenario gone bad really result in her friend's getting fired? If so, what would Lindsay do next? And would another school district be willing to hire her if this incident became part of her record? Lindsay had similar thoughts in her own apartment, though her thoughts had more of an urgency about them.

Questions for Consideration

1. What could Lindsay have done to prevent her current dilemma? What preestablished boundaries might have helped her make better choices?
2. Even if she had decided to break things off with Tom, why was confronting him in front of the school office a bad decision? How might she have handled this situation more professionally?
3. If the gender roles were reversed, how would this scenario change? Do you think a female administrator would receive the same number of

chances as Tom? What about a younger male teacher—would he have been in as much trouble as Lindsay? Why or why not?

4. Is it fair that Tom received a new position at district office—especially now that he had at least two such incidents on his record? What would you like to see a district do in a case like this?

5. Do the parents of the students have a right to be as concerned as they seem to be about what transpired? Why or why not? What other stakeholders might be upset by this type of relationship?

6. How would you advise a friend who wants to date someone at his or her job site? Do you have some ground rules you might recommend so that he or she could avoid problems down the road?

For Further Exploration

Example: When have I or someone I know ever had to deal with a dating dilemma at work? What happened during the course of the relationship? Were there any difficulties that had to be overcome?

Explanation: How would I best explain my dating policy to others—especially how I intend to implement it at work?

Exhortation: Are there some basic principles that I would encourage others to follow when it comes to beginning relationships with coworkers? How would I share this type of case study or a similar situation I have experienced to help someone else before he or she gets into trouble?

Environment: How can I best shield my students from problems that might occur due to my private life? Even if I'm not dating, will I be able to keep personal problems separate from how I interact with my kids—even if I've had a bad day?

Experience: What are some ways that I can encourage my students to learn the steps to good decision making when it comes to relationships with others? Even if many of their relationships may simply be at the friendship level, how can I help them learn to establish healthy boundaries in their lives?

CHAPTER THIRTEEN

~

Sex and the Single Teacher

Subdue your appetites, my dears, and you've conquered human nature.

—Charles Dickens, *Nicholas Nickleby*, 1838–1839

Initial Thoughts

Women have played many roles in developing the American educational system. Survey results taken from 1993 to 2004 reveal that approximately 75 percent of full-time teachers in the United States are female. Elementary schools tend to have the highest ratio of women to men, while the number becomes less striking in secondary schools, with a ratio of 56 percent female to 44 percent male (National Center for Educational Statistics 2007).

During the past two decades, women have more frequently assumed roles outside the classroom. From mentor teachers, to department chairs, to school administrators, to superintendents, female educators are in positions traditionally reserved mostly for men. Years ago, it was suggested that Dr. Infantino could easily become an elementary school principal, even though he had no elementary school experience. It seemed to be the fastest way to become a better-paid school district employee, an important consideration for someone with a young family. The person (a principal himself) indicated that Bob's lack of elementary experience didn't count as much as the fact that he was male. Today, thankfully, experience is an important factor for all jobs in the field of education for both sexes!

Interestingly, as women have assumed more positions of power, there have also been increased conflicts on some school campuses regarding these changes in authority figures. Sometimes these difficulties happen because male staff members are not willing to adjust to having a woman in charge. Early in her teaching career, Dr. Wilke observed several seasoned "professionals" on a middle school campus who tried regularly and rigorously to undermine the authority of a new female principal. The principal handled the situation gracefully and effectively, but one science teacher finally took early retirement because he simply could not deal with a woman at the helm of a twentieth-century school. Can you even imagine what he would think of all of the females in charge these days?

We have often observed gender-related issues occurring at larger, less personal high schools where the demands are intense and varied and the job of principal is quite stressful. However, gender-related interpersonal conflicts, though perhaps less frequent in smaller, mostly female-staffed elementary schools, often pose the same kinds of internal and external stressors for their principals.

The case below represents one such management issue: the personal and professional relationship between a newly hired male teacher and the principal of his school. You will find some similarities to the topics we have been discussing in past cases, but with new twists. First, there is a role reversal of traditional positions of power, with a female principal, a female department chair, and a young male teacher. Second, the woman seems to be the aggressor in the relationship, though you will have to decide if that is indeed the situation. Finally, both the males and females in this scenario face ethical decisions, and as we have read, the sexes sometimes view choices quite differently and often reach very different conclusions, in part due to gender-related perspectives.

Yet, the most significant issue to address is how the most personal of relationships, those involving sexual intimacy, impact all of the stakeholders in an educational setting. As we know, once the boundary of intimacy has been crossed, the professional relationship will indeed change as well. This is true whether you work at a bank or a small business, in a corporate setting or in a school district. As you read the following case study, think about how the couple's relationship might impact the students, parents, teachers, and other staff members.

The most basic of human needs—food, clothing, shelter, and love—must be met in order for one's life to be not only sustained but satisfying. *However, it is when these needs become of paramount importance that our ethics are tested at their deepest levels.* For instance, individuals who think that they would never consider stealing anything might be tempted to do so if they became homeless and hungry. The case study that follows demonstrates that where love is involved, boundaries can become fuzzy, and people sometimes do ridiculous things they would never have dreamed of doing before. This is particularly true when one who loves is injured . . . or even spurned.

Dickens's suggestion (or warning) from the well-known story above rings true for educators today, particularly for those whose careers may be jeopardized by their decisions. If we could indeed subdue and control those basest of our appetites, how much easier might life be? We will likely have fewer "tough choices" to make when it comes to relationships with those around us when we have put our basic needs in balance.

It will be interesting for you to discuss this case with your classmates, colleagues, and friends, especially as you discuss possible "ethical gender differences" as noted by Carol Gilligan (1993) in her research. Do today's newer teachers see any narrowing of the differences between ethical choices males and females make? Have you experienced any kinds of conflicts at school simply due to the ways gender differences influence ethical decisions?

As you read this case, remember to look once again at

- *Stakeholders:* Who will be affected by the actions of the characters in the scenario, and how will each stakeholder be altered by the characters' decisions?
- *Similar scenarios:* Have you ever encountered rumored relationships between educators as you attended school or college? Did those relationships have any impact on you personally or on the operations of the school?
- *Self-application:* If you happened to find yourself in the type of scenario that follows, what might you do similarly to or differently from the new teacher or his more experienced colleagues?

After reading this case, be sure to share your ideas with other people to get their opinions about the differing outcomes of these gender-based issues. It could make for some interesting and possibly *passionate* debates (pardon the expression, but we just couldn't resist in a chapter with this title).

Points to Ponder

Self-Application: What kind of boundaries have you set up in your interpersonal relationships? Are there ways you can protect your personal life from public view?

Case 11

Greenwood High School hired Reggie Greco, a newly certified, twenty-five-year-old science teacher. Mary Ann Gardner, the thirty-five-year-old, youthful-looking principal had divorced the previous school year and was attracted to Reggie from his initial interview. Ms. Gardner had a reputation around the school for making advances toward the male teachers, especially the younger ones. In fact, one of those past indiscretions had resulted in her divorce.

During the early part of the first semester, Reggie noticed that the principal was constantly around, helping him adjust to his assigned four periods of regular ninth-grade physical science and one period of a ninth- and tenth-grade life science for English Language Learners. Mary Ann offered Reggie advice about handling students and their parents, often complimenting both his abilities in the classroom and his attractive personal appearance. In November, Mary Ann asked Reggie to attend a local science lecture with her that would feature a renowned astronaut.

"Do you really think we should?" Reggie asked her, feeling a bit uncomfortable with how his coworkers might perceive this special treatment. After all, he was the newest staff member in the science department, so he thought someone with more seniority should probably go instead.

"Why not?" Mary Ann responded. "After all, I'm the one who gets to decide who attends these special events. Plus, you and I can spend some time getting to know each other better."

The two-hour lecture was followed by drinks at a local bar, then an overnight stay at a nearby hotel. Soon afterwards, Reggie and Mary Ann became an "item" around the school and in the school district, which was located in a moderately sized suburban city. Mary Ann and Reggie spent much of their free time together, including several weekends at a nearby resort owned by one of the school board members, Ralph Allant. A few colleagues had warned Reggie about Mary Ann's reputation, but Reggie seemed flattered by the attention of this older woman. After all, he knew of more and more couples comprising older women and younger men, so he felt that he would be able to handle this type of relationship pretty easily.

During the next few months, several parents complained to the district and the school board about the conduct of the couple, in addition to voicing their concern about the apparent poor teaching going on in Reggie's classes. In mid-February, Mary Ann and Reggie had a heated argument about their relationship. Reggie suggested strongly that they break the personal relationship off for a while and go back to the way things were at the beginning of the year. And so they did.

But Mary Ann, used to being in charge of all of her relationships, didn't like his rejection at all. In fact, she began to retaliate in small ways that soon became irritating to Reggie. At first, she simply ignored him when he said hello around campus. Then, materials he had requested from the custodian were either slow to arrive—or never made it at all. Reggie learned from Ryan Lee, a friend who worked in PE, that Mary Ann had the custodian "in her back pocket." If she didn't like someone, she told Mr. Combs to "make life difficult" for him or her. When Reggie didn't receive the television and DVD player he needed one day for his science classes, he marched to the office to speak to Mary Ann. Ms. Gardner's secretary informed Reggie that she was unavailable, and he would have to send her an e-mail about the problem.

In March, the school board had to decide whether to rehire Reggie, then a probationary science teacher, for the following year, since they had to notify teachers by March 15 about their status for September. So, the district administrators asked Mary Ann for a letter summarizing her evaluations of Reggie and for a recommendation about hiring him back. Mary Ann wrote a lengthy letter suggesting that perhaps the district should not rehire Reggie because of the frequent, though not vociferous, parental complaints about his poor teaching.

Ms. Gardner's letter read, in part, "Mr. Greco does have the potential to become a good teacher, but at this point, his shortcomings outweigh his abilities. Perhaps in another district he would relate better to the students and their parents. He is especially weak in teaching life science to the English Language Learners in his 9/10 class."

Meanwhile, Jane Garrison, the science department chair and mentor assigned to support and supervise Reggie, had observed many classes during the first semester of Reggie's teaching. Jane noted the typical mistakes made by rookie teachers, but she found nothing that couldn't be corrected with some effort on Reggie's part. Reggie was making that effort and his teaching was definitely improving. Jane had been aware of the rumored affair with the principal, but she wasn't sure at the time how to handle the situation. One thing she didn't want to do was get on Ms. Gardner's bad side. Once, during the midst of the rumored relationship, she'd asked Reggie if he wanted to discuss any personal issues in addition to his professional progress.

"Not really, Jane. Things are going great," Reggie had responded. "I think everybody considers me to be a good teacher, and I feel supported all the way up the line. But thanks for asking."

Later, Jane was relieved to hear about the couple's February breakup. During the year, other departmental and school colleagues had also exercised a hands-off policy, partially because they too feared reprisals from the principal.

Yet, several, including Reggie's friend Ryan, had urged Jane to try to intervene before things got out of hand. Too late!

One day in early March, Reggie received a phone call from a former college classmate who had been hired by a neighboring high school in the district. John Spencer informed Reggie of the rumors swirling about his affair and the breakup, and then John dropped this bombshell: "Reggie, I really struggled with whether I should call you or not about this—but I think you're going to get fired." John stated rather flatly: "Everyone I've talked to agrees that there's nothing much you can do about it."

Reggie, stunned by the revelation, asked about the sources of the statement. John merely said, "Believe me, it comes from people in the know."

Meanwhile, Jane wrote up a fairly positive, yet not excellent, evaluation of Reggie's teaching and professional responsibilities, one quite typical for a beginning teacher: "Mr. Greco has the potential to be a good teacher, and I feel that with some additional time and mentoring, he will do quite well. Besides, science teachers are hard to find, and he is a well-qualified candidate for retention after his first year." When Mary Ann asked her if she'd sent off a letter about Reggie to district office yet, Jane said she had and that she had indeed recommended that Reggie be retained for the next school year. Mary Ann didn't say a word to Jane, simply nodding her head before she left the classroom.

Well, Jane thought to herself, I'd better stock up on supplies. I have a feeling Mr. Combs won't be getting me the materials I need any time soon!

Ultimately, the school board, with resort-owner member Ralph Allant leading the majority decision, notified Reggie on March 15 that his contract would not be renewed for the following year. He would be terminated as of June 30.

Reggie was shocked. He ranted about the decision to his friend Ryan for over an hour after school that day, repeating over and over, "I can't believe that *she* would do this to me!" He also called John Spencer that night, still shaken by the bad news.

"Can't say I didn't warn you," his friend responded. "Nontenured teachers are really vulnerable and should stay out of potential trouble. Hey, at least you have time to look for a new job before fall."

But Reggie decided, on the advice of his teacher union's recommendation, to appeal the dismissal. He based the appeal on a "biased evaluation from the principal because of their broken off personal relationship." Citing his more positive evaluation from the department chair, Reggie wrote, "This action is a clear case of sexual harassment because of my personal and private connection to Ms. Gardner, and it is not related to my abilities in the classroom.

I ask for reconsideration of this action and reinstatement to my job for the next school year."

The school board contacted the principal and the department chair, neither of which suggested any changes to the comments they had already written. The board denied the appeal, citing laws concerning the dismissal of first- and second-year teachers without cause. Reggie was fired.

Questions for Consideration

Rather than contemplating a series of questions, for this case we would like you to do some role-play writing. Take a look at the characters listed for you below and select one. Review the person's actions in the case above. How might the person whose role you selected help to resolve this scenario? Write down a few notes about the case from that person's perspective, perhaps answering the questions posed below. You will be doing some sharing with others, so be prepared with written rationales that will help you remember your ethical decision-making process.

If You Were Reggie Greco

1. What would you do now? Why?
2. Are you at all to blame for your dismissal?
3. Should your private life, or any teacher's private life, be of concern to anyone else?

If You Were Mary Ann Gardner, the Principal

1. Did you do anything wrong here? Why or why not?
2. What ethical thinking processes should you have exercised in this case?
3. What should your position be if Reggie takes the case further, perhaps to a state or federal court?

If You Were Jane Garrison, the Department Chair

1. Why might you support Reggie in any further actions? Why might you not support him?
2. What ethical viewpoints could you call upon to guide your actions?
3. Would a department chair or mentor teacher be exercising proper ethical leadership if she intervened in the personal lives of the teachers under her guidance?

If You Were the Chair of the School Board

1. How can you ethically justify supporting the dismissal of Reggie Greco?
2. Why might you eventually oppose Ralph Allant's view about firing Reggie?
3. Under what conditions, if any, should an intimate relationship between colleagues, both consenting adults, be allowed?
4. Should the principal suffer any consequences in this case? If so, what consequences? If not, why?

The exercise of principled, ethical judgment seems to be generally absent in this case. Should guidelines be in place to discourage or prevent future incidents like this one? If you think so, could you write one such guideline?

For Further Exploration

Example: What example does such a relationship exhibit to my students and other students in the school? Do teachers have to be role models for their pupils? Should I be one?

Explanation: How would I explain my ethical decision-making process if I were in Reggie Greco's shoes? Can I make this an "it's okay" scenario?

Exhortation: High school students often have interpersonal issues related to the opposite sex. How should I deal with these issues if I work on a high school campus? How can I encourage fellow teachers to help kids resolve sexual issues? How do my values and background help ground me and allow me to show the way for young people?

Environment: Does my classroom have rules that guide students concerning interpersonal matters, particularly with regard to gender issues? What are those rules, and how should they be developed and implemented?

Experience: Am I willing to open gender-related issues for discussion in my classroom? Can I share stories or examples of people who have made strong ethical choices regarding relationships?

CHAPTER FOURTEEN

~

Character Matters

I have a dream that my four little children will one day live in a nation where they will not be judged by the color of their skin but by the content of their character.

—Dr. Martin Luther King Jr., "I have a dream" speech, 1963

Initial Thoughts

Personnel issues in staffing schools present some of the most vexing problems faced by all parties: district human resources offices, principals, teachers and school staffs, and the communities served by the school district. From initial hiring, to integration into teaching in the district, to continuing education, to retirement decisions, teachers seem to fall into two distinct groups: those who are low maintenance and those who are high maintenance.

Low-maintenance teachers are those who make a favorable impression in their initial interviews, who get assigned to schools and become part of the "the team," who are good with their students, cooperate in matters affecting others, and generally show character traits in their personal lives that will not affect their ability to teach their pupils well. They seem to get along quite well with others. This is not to say that such teachers are without problems. They may have family crises to deal with, their actions may be misconstrued by other people, they may not like one or more of their

117

colleagues, and so on. Generally speaking, low-maintenance people in all walks of life tend to be problem solvers rather than problem creators, and they seek appropriate advice and assistance when needed to help them address both personal and professional concerns.

High-maintenance teachers, on the other hand, are frequently seen during their initial interviews as having some "issues" that need resolution. Perhaps their collegiate records are not superb, their student-teaching evaluations are not of the highest level, or their interpersonal skills turn off some of the interviewers. They are often hired to meet a need that can't be filled by a more favorable person due to a shortage of candidates, a last-minute increase in the number of students arriving in the district, or a host of other reasons, including "they know somebody." Such high-maintenance teachers often create interpersonal problems among the staff. Their personal lives sometimes affect their classroom practices, they don't seem to follow rules well, or they tend to have problems coping with life in many other ways.

Interestingly, both high- and low-maintenance teachers often find their way to tenure in most districts. Even with the increased scrutiny of new teachers in their induction years, these high-maintenance educators manage to get enough positive evaluations to be granted tenure after two or three years, affording them needed security in retaining their positions, even if they subsequently do not perform as well as others think they should. Novice teachers sometimes "fly under the radar" for their first few years, and their problematic ways become openly evident only as their careers blossom or deteriorate in subsequent school terms.

One of your authors remembers a high school faculty meeting in which a new teacher, Allen, posed a question to the principal about a rule that he didn't think was appropriate. The principal, a former navy man, peered down his glasses at the young man with the question.

"Are you a first-year teacher?" the principal inquired.

"Yes, sir." Allen replied. "I'm just wondering why we have this rule in place. After all, we *are* adults."

"Well, just sit down and hold that question until you get tenure, will you," the principal retorted. "I make the rules around here. There are ways for you newbies to get your problems solved—and this meeting is not one of them."

The new teacher wasn't heard from much at faculty meetings after that, but he did manage to get tenure because he proved to be a good, low-maintenance teacher in subsequent months. We bet that Allen's ego was a bit deflated after the principal's chastisement, but at least he had the character to hold his ground and not let that incident negatively affect how he went about his business on campus.

Both low- and high-maintenance teachers experience personal problems from time to time. Everyone does. The low-maintenance teachers seem to cope better, even in the most difficult times, because of a better support system, a stronger will, or a strength of character that will not let them be defeated. They rarely let personal problems infiltrate their teaching or their relationships with students, parents, or coworkers.

High-maintenance teachers, on the other hand, often move from crisis to crisis, and, of course, everyone knows the status of the present crisis whether they want to or not. These "professionals" let personal issues permeate their entire lives, including their classroom time and adult time at school. Sometimes such educators become sullen or withdrawn when no one seems to care about their latest dilemma, and their teaching abilities drop in quality from that of better times.

Think about the high- and low-maintenance people that you have known. How did they impact your workplace or school environment? How did you deal with the high-maintenance people? Perhaps you could jot a few of these memories in your journal and share them with some classmates or coworkers this week as you process this chapter.

In the case that follows, you will meet several kinds of teachers, some of whom are high maintenance and others who are not. The first-year teacher involved here, Tina Carsoni, has to decide on a course of action that involves discussing the character of another teacher whom she knows fairly well. That older teacher has problems in need of resolution, but the district has apparently decided to shuffle the problem off to another school rather than confront a tenured veteran teacher.

Moving problem teachers from one school to another is a common practice, especially in larger districts with a strong teachers' association or union base. The trading of teachers for others who may also have unresolved problems in their respective schools has become known as "the dance of the lemons." It is a scenario in which each school agrees to exchange one teacher for another, hoping the problems of both will improve after the move. The public has scrutinized such shuffling more heavily in recent years, but the practice still seems prevalent.

As you read the case, consider the stakeholders involved and how the proposed decision to transfer the teachers affects each. In particular, consider how you, as a colleague of both teachers, should react when the "rumor mill" starts grinding out the news of impending moves.

Points to Ponder

As you take on additional roles and responsibilities in your career, the number of **Stakeholders** typically increases. You will have opportunities to draw on past **Similar Scenarios** to help you with new decisions that need to be made. Finally, the chances for **Self-Application**—particularly when it comes to the students in your care—will be of paramount importance.

Case 12

Tina Carsoni is a twenty-three-year-old new teacher at Public School (PS) 14 in a mid-sized urban district in the Northeast. Born in Argentina to American parents, she moved to the United States at the age of twelve. Much of her elementary education was done in Argentina, but her secondary and college schooling was completed in the United States. Tina attended a state college known for its innovative teacher-education programs. She spent two full semesters in preparation at PS 6, a professional-development partnership school, completing her field experiences and student-teaching semesters while taking classes on site. She worked as an aide for a semester and as a student teacher full-time for one semester in the primary-grade K–2 team.

In this latter setting, Tina met Maggie Cline, a fortyish second-grade teacher at PS 6. Maggie was a tenured, fifteen-year veteran teacher who was on the primary-grade team, and Tina worked as her second-grade classroom aide during the first semester of her field experiences.

Tina generally liked how Maggie taught her mostly African American students in a school about 75 percent composed of children of this ethnicity. But there were days when Tina regretted being part of Maggie's classroom. Often on Mondays, but increasingly on other days as well, Maggie would show up for work with bloodshot eyes and a haggard look. Rumors abounded concerning Maggie's weekend excesses. The word spread of her bar hopping, clubbing with different male companions each week, and very late-night or early-morning returns home. The problems started about two years before Tina arrived at the site, stemming from a broken relationship with a man Maggie had been dating for five years. As another staff member at school told Tina one day, "She's just never recovered from that heartbreak! She really thought he was the one."

At first, the issues didn't seem to affect Maggie's teaching very much. But as the semester wore on, Tina noted that the innovative reading program became filled more and more with worksheets and less and less with active story reading and writing activities. There was very little creativity on Mondays, and the rest of the week seemed awfully boring as well. Tina also noticed that the children's reading scores began falling on the biweekly assessments and that the students became restless during class time in all subjects. While most coworkers acknowledged Maggie's problems, no one seemed willing or able to tackle them.

During the second semester, Tina's student-teaching semester, a new principal was assigned to PS 6, Deeana Ingara, a middle-aged woman of Filipino descent. The district charged Ms. Ingara with instituting curricular reform, especially in reading and math in the primary grades, in order to improve national and state test scores and meet the federal and state standards for improvement each year.

At the first faculty meeting on the last Monday in January, Maggie Cline challenged the new principal about, as she put it, "top down reform." "What makes you think you can come in here and tell us how to teach?" Maggie snapped from her seat in the back row. "Many of us have been here a long time and know what's best for our kids, so just leave things alone."

"I am afraid that I can't do that, Ms. Cline," Ms. Ingara replied politely but firmly. "It seems that the school hasn't been performing up to the district's expectations, especially in the primary grades, and my challenge is to improve student performance. Several possibilities exist for all of us, including some additional teacher staff development and putting some present positions on the line next year."

"Well, we'll see about that," Maggie yelled as the meeting concluded. She stormed out the door, muttering to herself.

Things got worse from there. Tina was assigned to Sylvia Kenshaw for her student teaching, a fortunate placement in grade one of the same primary team. Sylvia, a fifty-four-year-old African American teacher with more than twenty-five years of experience, proved a perfect antidote to Maggie. She was a calming voice on the team, always encouraging Tina to be the best she could be, especially for the sake of the children.

In late February, Tina felt comfortable enough to approach Sylvia about Maggie's continuing problematic behaviors. "Leave it alone," Sylvia suggested gently. "Maggie is not your problem; this situation is for the principal and district to work out. Her antics are well known and will no doubt be addressed as soon as Ms. Ingara feels more confident about what to do about the many issues she is facing at this school."

So, Tina went along, surviving the semester, even consoling some of Maggie's students who came to her on those "bad Maggie days" when nothing seemed to go right. Tina tried to be helpful but feared that alcohol was affecting all aspects of Maggie's life—her teaching as well as her relationships with the kids, other staff, parents, the principal, and even district staff who had called her about her frequent Monday absences.

In June, the district offered Tina a position at PS 14 across town from her current school site. Glad to be moving to a new situation and getting rid of Maggie's problems, Tina went to meet with the primary teachers at her new school site. She was given the second-grade position she'd hoped for and vowed to herself not to emulate Maggie, except Maggie on the best days. She immediately observed that the school demographics were different from those at PS 6, with mainly Latino children of Puerto Rican and Central American backgrounds, from working-class families. Only about 10 percent of the pupils had African American or Caucasian backgrounds.

Tina felt very comfortable on this team and used her Spanish-language education to help ease her students' transition to English literacy. She had much success, as well as great support from her teammates and the school administration, and was able to implement many of the techniques she had learned in her own training.

In April of her first year at PS 14, Tina began to hear rumors about an impending teacher transfer for the next year, one that would affect her team. Michael Dodd, an African American first-grade teacher and an outspoken, tenured teacher of ten years, was to be transferred to PS 6, Tina's former school. He agreed to the transfer because it would put him closer to his basketball coaching position at the local high school. His absences for games and practices were a sore point for the principal of PS 14, as well as for the parents and the other staff members who had to cover for him at least three times a week during the season. In addition, some parents had expressed concern with his openness about his Muslim faith.

In exchange for Michael Dodd, PS 14 was to receive none other than Maggie Cline. This seemed a clear case of "the dance of the lemons," as a coworker explained it to Tina, the trading of one unwanted or problematic teacher for another. Though their issues were different, both Maggie and Michael faced the choice of a transfer or a disciplinary action due to the effects of their problems on their teaching, their pupils, and their colleagues. Both accepted the new assignments, Michael eagerly . . . Maggie bitterly.

Now Tina wondered what to do. Should I speak to my principal about Maggie? Maybe I can talk generally to the primary-grade team leader, Phyllis, and see what she thinks first. One afternoon, Tina headed for Phyllis Thomas's room right after school.

"Leave it alone," warned Phyllis. "Stay out of the politics for your first few years, at least until you have tenure. You can never be sure who knows whom in this profession. It's best to lay low for right now, Tina, while you're still new here. But I appreciate the heads-up about Maggie."

Tina decided to call Anita Brenman, a former college colleague who was now working at PS 6, to check up on Maggie's activities. Anita reported that things were worse than before with Maggie. Lots of complaints had been made by parents and kids. Yet, Anita was also matter-of-fact in her summary of the whole situation: "Everybody needs a change, Tina. It's really hard to fire or discipline a tenured teacher. Maybe the lemon exchange would be good for all concerned." Tina scowled to herself on the other end of the line.

Tina thought again about speaking to her principal, Alfredo Ramirez, but all her teammates advised against it. She even asked the teachers' association representative, but he also advised a "hands-off" policy.

Yet, Tina just could not bear the thought of another year on the same school staff, much less on the same team, with Maggie Cline. She figured that she might have to ask for a transfer herself, but there were few openings in the district, and tenured teachers had first choice to bid on the better positions. Besides, transfers before a tenure decision were not very common unless the teacher herself was a problem worth salvaging.

The May 15 staffing deadline for the following September was fast approaching. Tina faced several tough choices: Maybe I should join my friends for happy hour tonight and run some of these issues by them. Or I could just leave it alone like everyone keeps saying and simply stick out another year with Maggie—and maybe hope for some sort of divine intervention!

Questions for Consideration

1. Can you outline in your mind the dilemmas Tina faces? What factors must she consider? Who are the stakeholders affected by each of these factors? Should Tina's concern for her students outweigh the other issues, even her personal happiness?

2. Why does "the Dance of the Lemons" seem an inappropriate way to deal with tenured teachers' underperformance? What might be some other solutions when veteran teachers let personal problems interfere with professional performance? Do school districts and teachers' associations have any responsibility to assist? Why or why not?

3. We all have flaws in our personal makeup; you can see many of them displayed by the characters involved in this and the preceding cases. Yet, strength of character seems to be important for all teachers. So,

how does one develop such strengths as courage, loyalty, trustworthiness, and honesty, especially in the face of others who don't exhibit these characteristics?

4. What should Tina do to resolve the dilemmas she's dealing with? What elements of good decision making would you recommend to her to resolve this scenario?
5. Who are the low-maintenance educators in this case study? Who are the high-maintenance ones? What could the latter do to improve their performance at their current school sites?
6. How can you avoid becoming a "lemon" in your professional career—to your students, parents, or fellow staff members? What *intentional efforts* are you willing to put forth to ensure that you'll keep striving to be an exceptional educator—and human being?

For Further Exploration

Example: Bringing personal problems to the workplace never seems appropriate, yet many people do just that! What can I do to avoid becoming like them and letting my personal problems affect my teaching life?

Explanation: Tina tried to assist Maggie's pupils when they brought their problems to her. How might I handle such a situation delicately, without turning away the students or undermining their teacher? How could I talk about this problem with the teacher involved?

Exhortation: Teachers of character need to demonstrate those virtues to others constantly and consistently. I will always be "on stage" as a teacher, even when I'm out in the community. How can I remind myself of this truth, and how should I encourage my colleagues also to be good representatives while in the community at large?

Environment: Foundation textbooks often tell us that American public schools were begun for the dual purpose of building an educated citizenry and forming people of good character. If I believe in these two principles, what kind of classroom environment should I maintain, especially to promote good character and good decision making?

Experience: In my K–12 experiences thus far, have I noticed teachers whose personal problems seem to affect their teaching? Without revealing identities or specific school sites, can I share some of these observations with others in order to gain their input on the situations? How might the problematic experiences of others add to my ability to resolve my problems and make better choices in the future?

Epilogue

Now that you have read the cases and reacted to them, how are you feeling about ethical challenges in today's schools and classrooms? We are sure that your experiences and insights, along with those of your instructors and classmates, have provided lively and thoughtful discussions. We hope that you went back into the chapter about the various approaches to ethical decision making to see if your problem-solving strategies fit one or more of the classic definitions or are being influenced by people and events in your upbringing. If you have not yet done so, now is a good time for such a review.

While recently watching the movie *Freedom Writers* (Gruwell 1999), we were struck by the response of character Miep Gies, the woman who sheltered Anne Frank and her family during World War II and who discovered and preserved Anne's diary. Addressing a high school student who called her a hero, Gies replied, "I'm no hero. I did what I had to do. It was the right thing to do." She spoke like a true Kantian thinker, one who acts for the sake of duty.

That story is indeed from the real world, as are the scenarios in the cases you have worked on. We hope that as you go further into your career as educators, you will recall how you looked at the problems faced by the newer teachers in these case studies. Perhaps you will become more caring in your decision making; perhaps you will weigh the consequences for all the stakeholders more often; or perhaps you will come to understand the benefits of acting for the sake of duty as Miep Gies did.

The real world of ethical decision making, however, is often fast and furious, providing neither the luxury of time nor the opportunity for long-term reflection. So, developing good character qualities and habits of sound decision making right now will actually serve as a type of insurance policy against rashness and unethical practices. We provide you with one more opportunity to test your skills in appendix A.

Best wishes to you all. May you have as fruitful and rewarding careers as we have had during our many years in the profession. Thank you for choosing to touch the future by teaching the next generation of young people!

~

Appendix A

Helping Student Athletes or Helping Students with Special Needs: An Ethical Dilemma

In this appendix, we present you with an opportunity to enact a role-play about an educational problem. It is a chance to put into practice the decision-making skills you have been reading, writing, and talking about. When we tried out this scenario with college students, we found that the more they "got into character," the more interesting the scenario became. You will need to use your powers of persuasion, summarize your own "points to ponder" within an allocated time, and react civilly, as though you were attending an actual meeting of a local education board. We hope that the enactment will be both an educational and entertaining experience for all of you.

The Role-playing Scenario

The community and school district of Fairfield, Oklahoma, have a decision to make. The elected school board has to decide between building a state-of-the-art gymnasium to replace one that is fifty-five years old with warped floors from the previous year's floods or building a state-of-the-art classroom facility for, and accessible to, the many handicapped students in this single high school district. No such facility exists at present, and these handicapped pupils are attending classes in a converted storage building. The state education department is pressuring the school district to provide a better facility for these high schoolers.

The community passed a bond issue for $7 million, enough to provide either the new gym or the new facility for the handicapped, but not both. Additional local monies will not be available for at least five years, and the state and federal governments are unable to lend any help because of the recessionary economy and the existing political situation between the state and federal levels.

Many student athletes are pushing for the new gym since their future college scholarships and, ultimately, their athletic careers may depend on playing in a decent facility without getting injured. The handicapped students and their parents are also pressuring the school board since their educational lives, future happiness, and potential careers are in serious jeopardy, given the present facility. Teachers' views seem mixed.

The Board of Education meeting is next week, and you will have the opportunity to act out this scenario with your classmates. Once you are assigned a role, each of you will have up to two minutes to make a presentation to the board explaining your point of view. You should write a few notes in advance to remind yourself about what to say. You can certainly research the issue independently and incorporate any of your findings into your presentation.

At presentation time, you must first identify yourself and state your role; then, you will explain the morality of the issue from your given perspective. Finally, you can state your own position as forcefully as you'd like. You might try to draw an analogy to a similar problem you have noted in other districts. Be sure to define your terms and make necessary moral distinctions. Try to be rational, yet stand by your position even if it is an emotional argument.

Board members will first either briefly express their own tentative positions or offer no position at all. They will then listen to other participants' presentations, discuss the issues among themselves, and take a public vote on which course of action to take. Board members may stand by their initial positions or change their minds as the meeting goes along. The board president maintains order. The superintendent recognizes and invites the speakers to the podium. The board secretary informs speakers of their time limits, giving a twenty-second warning as well. In the interest of getting things decided and voted on by the end of the class session, only one question from the board members, directed through the board president, may be asked of each presenter. We have found that 1.5 to 2 hours is sufficient time for the role-play enactment.

Roles for the Participants in the Simulation

The list below indicates the various roles to be assigned by the instructor and the order of the presentations. Each speaker is limited to *two minutes or less*, with the time monitored and notes kept by the board secretary. Each speaker is invited up to the front by the superintendent. No one speaks from the audience seats. The speaker gives his or her real name and explains to the board members the role he or she is representing.

Only the first twelve roles are necessary, although the number of board members may be reduced to five if participant numbers are low. The board secretary does not vote. The remaining roles should be selected from the rest of the list, balancing the number and types of presentations that might be expected in a fair school board hearing.

We have not specified the nature of the testimony expected by the role-players; thus, participants are free to prepare their testimony as they see fit, based on their best ethical and educational thinking. Each person should address the board members directly, not the audience. However, remarks made by previous speakers may certainly be supported or rebutted in the testimony.

After the presentations and vote, the instructor or coordinator should lead a debriefing of the process, the discussions, and the outcome. Class participants should be able to express their feelings, explain their ethical decision-making rationales, state their confusions, and bring out other aspects related to the role-play scenario.

The Roles

1. School board president
2. Board member
3. Board member
4. Board member
5. Board member
6. Board member
7. Board member
8. Board secretary
9. Superintendent of schools
10. Mayor of Fairfield
11. President of the Fairfield Teachers Association
12. Chief plant engineer/head custodian
13. Special education teacher who supports funding the special education building
14. Special education teacher who does not support funding the special education building
15. Head of the physical education department
16. Physical education teacher
17. Head counselor

18. Counselor of academically gifted students
19. College professor of special education
20. Wheelchair-bound athlete
21. Captain of the baseball/softball team
22. Blind student who is president of the Associated Student Body
23. Special education graduate who is employed in business world
24. President of the Parent-Teacher Association
25. Chair of the athletic supporters
26. Mother of a child with cerebral palsy
27. State education department representative
28. College volleyball player and Fairfield graduate
29. Public citizen, head of Taxpayers against Kids and Education
30. Construction company owner looking for a building contract

~

Appendix B

Recommended Readings for
Educators about Ethics and Values

Boylan, M., and J. A. Donahue. 2003. *Ethics across the curriculum: A practice-based approach*. Lanham, MD: Lexington Books.

Carter, H. L., T. S. Foulger, and A. D. Ewbank. 2008. Have you googled your teacher lately? Teachers' use of social networking sites. *Phi Delta Kappan* 89, no. 9: 681–85.

Character Education Partnership, at www.character.org.

Cloud, H. 2006. *Integrity: The courage to meet the demands of reality*. New York: HarperCollins.

Center for Ethics in Society at Standard University at http://ethicsinsociety.stanford.edu.

Gardner, R. 2003. *Education for values: Morals, ethics and citizenship in contemporary teaching*. New York: Routledge Falmer.

Ethics Newsline at the Institute for Global Ethics at www.globalethics.org/newsline/?s+kidder.

Infantino, R. 1989. Moral challenges in education. *California English* 25 (4) (September/October): 24–25.

———. 1994. The ethical dimensions of leadership. President's Column. *California English* 30 (3) (fall).

Johns, B. H., M. Z. McGrath, and S. R. Mathur. 2008. *Ethical dilemmas in education: Standing up for honesty and integrity*. Lanham, MD: Rowman & Littlefield Publishers.

Keith-Spiegel, P., B. E. Whitley, D. W. Balogh, D. V. Perkins, and H. F. Wittig. 2002. *The ethics of teaching: A casebook*. 2nd ed. Upper Saddle River, NJ: Lawrence Erlbaum.

Lickona, T. 2004. *Character matters: How to help our children develop good judgment, integrity, and other essential virtues*. New York: Touchstone.

Mahoney, D. 2008. *Ethics in the classroom: Bridging the gap between theory and practice*. Lanham, MD: Rowman & Littlefield Publishers.

Ryan, K., and K. E. Bohlin. 2003. *Building character in schools: Practical ways to bring moral instruction to life*. San Francisco: Jossey-Bass.

Silverman, R., W. M. Welty, and S. Lyon. 1995. *Case studies for teacher problem solving*. 2nd ed. New York: McGraw-Hill.

Strike, K. A. 2006. *Ethical leadership in schools: Creating community in an environment of accountability*. Thousand Oaks, CA: Corwin Press.

Strike, K. A., and J. F. Soltis. 2004. *The ethics of teaching*. 4th ed. New York: Teacher's College Press.

Appendix C
Recommended Resources for Today's Teachers

Armstrong, T. 2000. *Multiple intelligences in the classroom*. 2nd ed. Alexandria, VA: Association for Supervision and Curriculum Development.

Cloud, H. 1997. *Changes that heal: How to understand the past to ensure a healthier future*. Grand Rapids, MI: Zondervan Publishing House.

———. 2004. *Nine things you simply must do to succeed in love and life*. Nashville, TN: Thomas Nelson.

Kidder, T. 1989. *Among schoolchildren*. Boston: Houghton Mifflin Company.

Linn, R., and M. D. Miller. 2005. *Measurement and assessment in teaching*. 9th ed. Upper Saddle River, NJ: Pearson Merrill Prentice Hall.

Marzano, R. J. 2006. *Classroom assessment & grading that work*. Alexandria, VA: Association for Supervision and Curriculum Development.

McCourt, F. 2005. *Teacher man: A memoir*. New York: Scribner.

Meier, D. 1995. *The power of their ideas*. Boston: Beacon Press.

Nieto, S. 1999. *The light in their eyes: Creating multicultural learning communities*. New York: Teachers College Press.

O'Connor, K. 2002. *How to grade for learning: Linking grades to standards*. 2nd ed. Thousand Oaks, CA: Corwin Press.

Palmer, P. J. 2007. *The courage to teach: Exploring the inner landscape of a teacher's life*. 10th anniv. ed. San Francisco, CA: Jossey-Bass.

Peck, M. S. 2003. *The road less traveled, 25th anniversary edition: A new psychology of love, traditional values and spiritual growth*. New York: Touchstone.

Pitch, B., and T. Quinn. 2006. *Real-time problem solving in schools: Case studies for school leaders*. Lanham, MD: Rowman & Littlefield Publishers.

Ryan, K., and J. Cooper. 2004. *Those who can, teach.* 10th ed. Boston: Houghton Mifflin Company.

Wilke, R. 2005. *Improving teaching and learning: What's your relationship quotient?* Lanham, MD: Rowman & Littlefield Publishers.

———. 2005. *The first days of class: A practical guide for the beginning teacher.* Thousand Oaks, CA: Corwin Press.

References

Agnes, M., and D. B. Guralnik, eds. 2007. *Webster's new world college dictionary.* 4th ed. Cleveland, OH: Wiley Publishing.

Banks, J. A. 2005. *Cultural diversity and education: Foundations, curriculum, and teaching.* 5th ed. Boston: Allyn and Bacon.

Boutte, G. S. 2002. *Resounding voices: School experiences of people from diverse ethnic backgrounds.* Boston: Allyn and Bacon.

Cloud, H., and J. Townsend. 1992. *Boundaries: When to say yes, when to say no to take control of your life.* Grand Rapids, MI: Zondervan Publishing House.

———. 1995. *Safe people: How to find relationships that are good for you and avoid those that aren't.* Grand Rapids, MI: Zondervan Publishing House.

De Roche, E., and M. M. Williams. 2001. *Educating hearts and minds: A comprehensive character education framework.* 2nd ed. Thousand Oaks, CA: Corwin Press.

Dead poets society. 1989. Directed by Peter Weir. Touchstone Pictures.

Frymier, J., L. Cunningham, W. Ducket, B. Gansneder, F. Link, J. Rimmer, and J. Schultz. 1995. *Values on which we agree.* Bloomington, IN: Phi Delta Kappa International.

Gilligan, C. 1993. *In a different voice: Psychological theory and women's development.* Cambridge, MA: Harvard University Press.

Gruwell, Erin. 1999. *The freedom writers diary.* New York: Random House (basis for Paramount Pictures' January 2007 movie *Freedom Writers*).

Hinman, L. M. 2008. *Ethics: A pluralistic approach to moral theory.* 4th ed. Belmont, CA: Wadsworth Publishing.

Huffman, H. A. 1994. *Developing a character education program: One school district's experience.* Alexandria, VA: Association for Supervision and Curriculum Development.

Hunter, J. D. 2000. *The death of character: Moral education in an age without good or evil*. New York: Basic Books.

Infantino, R. 1996. Who decides what you teach? President's Perspective. *California English* 6 (winter).

Jensen, R. A., and T. J. Kiley. 2000. *Teaching, leading, and learning: Becoming caring professionals*. Boston: Houghton Mifflin.

Josephson, M. S. 2002. *Making ethical decisions*. Los Angeles, CA: Josephson Institute of Ethics.

Kidder, R. M. 2003. *How good people make tough choices: Resolving the dilemmas of ethical living*. New York: Harper.

Kohlberg, L. 1981. *The philosophy of moral development: Moral stages and the idea of justice*. Essays on Moral Development 1. New York: Harper & Row.

McCullough, D. 2001. *John Adams*. New York: Simon & Schuster.

Moore, G. E. 1998. *Principia ethica*. Paris: University Presses of France.

National Center for Education Statistics. 2007. *Contexts of elementary and secondary education, 2007*. Indicator 33. www.nces.ed.gov/programs/coe (accessed June 10, 2008).

Noddings, N. 1984. *Caring: A feminine approach to ethics and moral education*. Berkeley, CA: University of California Press.

———. 2002. *Educating moral people: A caring alternative to character education*. New York: Teacher's College Press.

Ornstein, A. C., and D. U. Levine. 2007. *Foundations of education*. 10th ed. Boston: McGraw-Hill.

Peck, M. S. 1998. *People of the lie: The hope for healing human evil*. 2nd ed. New York: Touchstone.

Queen, J. A., J. R. Burrell, and S. L. McManus. 2001. *Planning for instruction: A yearlong guide*. Columbus, OH: Prentice Hall.

Rawls, J. 2005. *A theory of justice: Original edition*. Cambridge, MA: Belknap Press.

Ryan, K. 1986. The new moral education. *Phi Delta Kappan* 68, no. 4: 228–33.

Wong, H. K., and R. T. Wong. 1998. *The first days of school: How to be an effective teacher*. Mountain View, CA: Harry K. Wong Publications.

About the Authors

Robert Infantino, EdD, recently completed forty-three years in education, retiring in 2007 as professor emeritus from the University of San Diego (USD). Educated at Canisius College in Buffalo, New York, with a doctorate in English education from the University of Buffalo, Dr. Infantino was a high school English teacher and department chair in the Buffalo public schools. He then served as director of teacher education at USD for more than twenty years. His teaching included the course "Ethics and Education," cotaught with his colleague Dr. Larry Hinman, director of the USD Values Institute. Dr. Infantino has served as codirector of the San Diego Area Writing Project, as president of the California Association of Teachers of English, and as a member of several professional boards. Five of his six children and one grandchild are also teachers. In retirement, Dr. Infantino continues to make presentations on ethics, assessment, and the teaching of writing. He can be reached at infantino@sandiego.edu.

Rebecca Wilke, EdD, served as a teacher and a university professor, as well as an educational and leadership consultant, working with children and adults in both public and private school settings for over twenty years. At the University of Southern California, Dr. Wilke specialized in educational leadership and multicultural education. Currently she is president of LEADon Inc., a leadership-development company based in San Diego, California. Dr. Wilke has also authored two previous books for beginning teachers and experienced educators. She can be reached at www.leadon.biz or via e-mail at doctorswilke@cox.net.